HE STRATO R CONTINUES

ISBN-13: 978-1-4950-0455-1
ISBN-10: 0-634-05613-1

Published by:
Hal Leonard Corporation
7777 W. Bluemound Road
P.O. Box 13819
Milwaukee, WI 53213

Library of Congress Cataloging-in-Publication Data has been applied for.

Printed in USA

First Edition

Visit Hal Leonard Online at **www.halleonard.com**

Book Design by Richard Slater

On the cover:
Eric Johnson Stratocaster in Dakota Red, with a bound rosewood fingerboard.

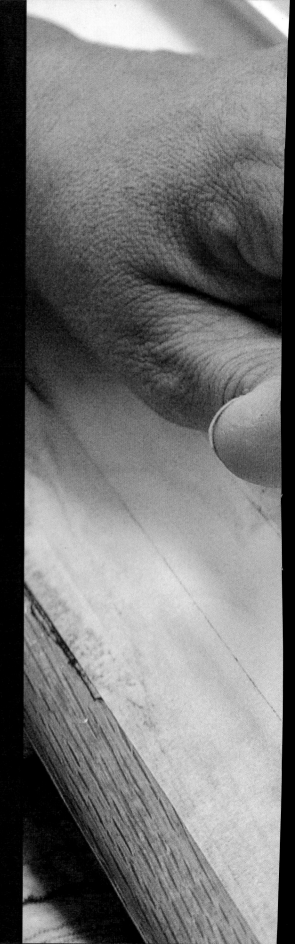

INTRODUCTION

There is nothing on earth like a Fender Stratocaster—this piece of wood with strings and wires and a few parts of plastic and metal, this … *thing*, this most animate of supposedly inanimate objects. There might not be many active musicians who remember when this 60-year-old icon was spankin' new, but there are a great many who remember when it was new for them, who remember their discovery of a guitar like no other.

I spent about three years writing *The Stratocaster Chronicles*, which in 2004 commemorated the guitar's 50th anniversary. Excerpts from that book's Introduction:

Could the same instrument that once appeared so radical it made people wonder if it were actually a guitar have had so profound an influence over the past half-century that, somehow, it has come to epitomize the public's idea of what an electric guitar looks like, what an electric guitar *is*? Well, yes. But how did that happen? Simply put, Mr. Fender considered existing products, saw flaws, thought he could do better, and went ahead and did it. The outcome was an instrument so far ahead of its time that other manufacturers' models—even some that came along years later—looked stodgy by comparison.

I've come to think that Mr. Fender's status as a non-player and industry outsider was an advantage, because it freed him from orthodoxy, gave him a blank slate. Could anyone, no matter how brilliant, have dreamed up the Stratocaster if he had been rooted in established notions of how electric guitars looked, sounded, and were supposed to work?

While the Stratocaster is still Mr. Fender's guitar in terms of its design and construction, in other respects the incandescent, unruly offspring slipped away from its father a long time ago. Indeed, the ingenuity of the Strat's inventor is only the beginning of its story; the rest is found in the boundless creativity of the players who picked it up and plugged it in. As if taking their cue from Leo himself, some of the players who adopted his Stratocaster redefined it to suit their visions, as Mr. Fender had redefined the electric guitar to suit his own.

Inheriting a romanticized legacy of innovation, commercial revolution, and the groundbreaking artistry of fabled musicians is a tough gig. Legacy is at once a privilege and a burden. You can't stand still. You have to change—but not too much. Unveiling new Stratocasters is all about drawing fine lines and a thoughtful, sometimes risky balance of competing considerations. *The Stratocaster Continues* updates *The Stratocaster Chronicles* and reflects the strategies and inspirations of designers and marketers who carry forth the storied legacy of a once and future radical guitar into a new age of shifting tastes, global markets, social media, and digital technologies.

Special thanks to Eric Johnson, whom I have admired since his days as a local Austin hero in the Electromagnets. The thoughtfulness, soulfulness, and precision of his foreword will likely surprise no one who knows his music.

Starting my research almost four decades ago, I was fortunate to interview most of the people who founded Fender and created its instruments. All were generous with their time. Company executives, marketers, designers, and builders continue to support my efforts to interpret the significance of their guitars, basses, and amps and to discover and recount the stories behind the creation and impact of those instruments. Special thanks to current and former Fender folk John Cruz, Mike Eldred, Greg Fessler, Ritchie Fliegler, Michael Frank-Braun, Mark Kendrick, Todd Krause, Mike Lewis, Richard McDonald, Justin Norvell, Yuriy Shishkov, Jason Smith, Larry Thomas, Paul Waller, and Dale Wilson.

Writers like to think that people will actually read our work, but we know that to the bookstore browser, it's the images that catch the eye. I very much appreciate the contributions of photographers Eric Fairchild, Mark Keraly, Dave Maddux, Steve Pitkin, and Matt York, as well as proofreaders Anna Bird, Hannah Golden, and Isabel Zacharias. Thanks also to hand-engraver Tim Adlam; designer, inventor, and President of Fishman Transducers, Inc. Larry Fishman; artist Frank Germano of Man On Fire Design; retailer Howard Gillespie of Oasis Musical Instruments, Ltd., Ringwood, Hampshire, UK; guitarist/columnist Joe Gore; artist manager Joe Priesnitz; and designer Ian St.John-White of VML, Northwood, Middlesex, UK.

I am so fortunate to be on Hal Leonard's team with Vice President Creative Services Richard Slater, who designed and named this book, Senior Sales and Marketing Manager Brad Smith, and Editor J. Mark Baker. Thanks for giving me so many opportunities and for making my books look so good.

Thanks to Anne, Joe, Matt, and Dan for your love and support. I count my blessings every day.

— Tom Wheeler, 2014

"The whole guitar was pretty good."

— Leo Fender

"There is a sacred geometry to everything, including making guitars."

– Eric Johnson

The Serendipitous Grace of Alchemy

by Eric Johnson

I was at a friend's house when I was about 10 years old. He had a Fender catalog from 1964 full of Strats and Dual Showmans and Twin Reverbs, and it was the coolest thing I ever saw. I remember being out to dinner once, about that same age, and there was a band playing in a supper club. I distinctly remember the guy had a white Fender, either the Jazzmaster or Jaguar, and he leaned it up against the amp during intermission. I went over there to look at it. I just stood there. *Oh my God, look at that!*

I wish I'd had a chance to meet Leo Fender. I would have asked him if he thought some of the best ideas came naturally and serendipitously, rather than sweating over them too much, and I would commend him for standing by the artistry and musicality of his work, which was so pivotal. It wasn't about how many beans they could count or where the market share was. I would commend him for his integrity. I would ask him about the changes he made over the years, and what his thought process was. I think you would have to be an intuitive genius to do what he did, to pick up this energy around you and manifest it somehow in the real world.

I do think there is a sacred geometry to everything, including making guitars and amps and everything else on this plane. I think if we had some balcony view we could look out and it would look like a mandala or a big lotus flower that was symmetrical and somehow universally simple. But we're down here on the ground in the everyday world, and from this point of view, things look so complicated we would have to live 800 or 900 years to even approach figuring it all out.

But there are some things we do know. Some things are a must in order to get the great guitar that will deliver you to your destination, so you can go to that outer sphere of pushing the envelope. People have subjective ideas about what a great instrument is, but for me, I've distilled it down to a guitar with resonant wood, well-made pickups, tuning stability, and a neck that affords you the right posturing to where you can play nice chord voicings as well as leads.

Being picky about details is important, but there has to be a balance. Thinking about details can help you get to a point where you have a superlative sound and a reliable instrument, but if you have all of those basics, then does it really get much better? I've chased those details sometimes, but now I try to realize that getting all the basics just right might be as good as it gets. That's where all the magic is anyhow. You can get lost in this abyss. The mind comes into play–*what if the grain patterns were a little closer together, or what if they were a little further apart, or the guitar weighed a half-pound less? Would that make it better?* You can get into a vicious cycle, a rabbit hole, and you don't make it better. You just go sideways.

Leo Fender took care of so much of this stuff with the Stratocaster's first edition, in 1954. Some of the best guitars I've ever played were from that very first year. Sometimes that initial, inspired, intuitive manifestation gets everything pretty darn close. If you get 94 percent of everything right the first time, you can spend the next 40 years trying to get to 94.3.

I could say that having my own signature Stratocaster is a dream come true, but it's more than that. Sometimes

I still can hardly believe it. It's actually kind of surreal to see my ideas put into effect by Fender and somebody so brilliant as Michael Frank-Braun. People have told me that some of the ideas from our signature guitar project have been adopted in other Fenders, and I think there might be something to that, because I think Fender is making the best pickups they've made since the '60s. The guitars are really good. I got one of their reissue 60th Anniversary '54 Strats, and it's a great guitar.

To make great guitars, tiny little things do make a difference, so it's good to explore all this. It's not always the big glaring things. But eventually, as a musician, you arrive at the point of letting go. That secret exists, but it exists serendipitously. You get a guitar and every single piece is just right, but it's more a matter of interconnectivity, how all the parts fit together. It has to do with nature and the serendipitous grace of alchemy. I think that in the bigger picture, you just want to pick up the guitar and play.

I found my way to the Stratocaster. It's such a versatile guitar. It's my go-to instrument. It delivers. It's the best candidate for going as many places as possible. You know, we are not in charge of everything. We are powerless in a way. This whole thing is way bigger than us. So at this point, I just try to surf the magic. A big wave comes in, and I try to have gratitude for that wave. I can't create it. It comes in and it's 12 feet. I've learned to not sit there and say I want a 14-foot wave. Go ride that wave.

Eric Johnson

The Commemorative Stratocaster is one of seven new models released in celebration of the Strat's 60th anniversary.

A Decade of Change
Pride Resurrected, and a Move Home

Justin Norvell joined Fender in 1995, working in R&D, sales, and other areas. After serving as marketing manager for Squier, he took over leadership of Fender's guitar department—for nearly seven decades the soul and the financial cornerstone of the company. He spearheaded the development of acclaimed models such as the 50th Anniversary Jazzmaster, the über-versatile Fender/Roland VG Strat, the vibey Road Worn series, several artist signature models, and the Squier '51 of the mid-2000s—nothing less than one of the greatest bang-for-the-buck electric guitars of all time. His current title is Vice President of Marketing for Electric Guitars.

Richard McDonald started at Fender answering the phones as a parts-department clerk. Over the years, the company recognized that his combination of business savvy, people skills, and deep grasp of the Fender brand (not to mention considerable prowess on the guitar) made him an ideal candidate for leadership roles. After heading up the separate marketings of Fender amps and Fender guitars, he progressed through a series of promotions to the position of Executive Vice President, directing the marketing of the entire Fender brand.

Larry Thomas is the former President, CEO, and Chairman of retail giant Guitar Center. He became Fender's CEO in August 2010 and retired in 2014. He inherited a company that, like many others, struggled to survive amid a calamitous economic recession marked by, among other downturns, drastic cutbacks in consumer spending. As a backdrop to explaining the strategy behind the design and manufacture of new Strats and other models, he offers a recap of his three-plus years at the top.

Very few people can offer the dual perspective of a serious guitarist and successful top executive, but Justin Norvell, Richard McDonald, and Larry Thomas all fit the bill. Here, they look back over the decade since the first edition of this book was published, detailing the development of new models and explaining fundamental shifts in the market, and at Fender.

Richard McDonald: In the ten years since the original *Stratocaster Chronicles* came out, our world has changed a lot. International trends have continued to evolve. There's been a lot of rebalancing across manufacturing, due to global economics. First we were in Japan, but the yen goes in the other direction and you lose your value there, so then we're in Korea, but then that doesn't work as well, then Indonesia. Some places once had incredible labor efficiencies, like China, but labor rates there have gone up dramatically. There's been movement and resettling as middle classes have emerged in a lot of these manufacturing countries.

With a product manufactured offshore, you take into consideration the 30 days it spends on the water, communication issues, time differences, language barriers that can create misunderstandings and mistakes—you start netting all that out and the result is, in short, a move home. Our facility in Ensenada, Mexico feels like a home base, just like the main factory in Corona, California. I can drop the phone here in Scottsdale and be in Ensenada in a couple of hours. When analyzing transportation costs between our two hometown facilities, we think, wow, we can make even more great USA-made and Ensenada-made products. Now, we have to have a really, really good reason to build something in a place other than our own bases in Corona and Ensenada.

Larry Thomas: Before I got there, they had very serious quality-control issues with the guitars. Richard McDonald looked into it and found all sorts of problems. He went to my predecessor and said, look, we can't do this, this has to stop, so the CEO shut down the factory, totally. This was about April of 2010. We also had a fiasco with our paint; we had to get new suppliers. I was familiar with these problems because I was on Fender's board before becoming CEO. So, some people were fired, and they brought [Senior VP of Global Manufacturing] Sergio Villanueva up from the Ensenada facility to run the factory. Mark Kendrick, from the Custom Shop, was a huge help in the factory with quality control.

When I arrived, I discovered the two worlds of Fender: the Scottsdale group, where the leadership and brainpower was with sales and marketing, and then the Corona factory, where people were expected to do what they were told. But I liked going to the factory. It's such a dynamic place, and my feeling was, we are guitar makers. We need to unleash innovation there because a lot of these workers have great ideas. Back in the day, the manufacturers' offices were all in the factories. Ted McCarty had an office in Chicago, but he was at Gibson in Kalamazoo all the time. Today, too:

Paul Smith at PRS, Bob Taylor, Chris Martin—I thought to myself, this is crazy. I'm not a manufacturer, but I do have an eye for product, and I knew Leo was in the thick of it every day. His office was right there on the production floor. I thought maybe that's the key. The executives need to be closer to the factory.

RM: We realized that the most important thing in the world to us is right on the factory floor in Southern California. We've reconsidered our legacy. We look at the Stratocaster and think, my gosh, this instrument has gone from Buddy Holly to Bob Dylan going electric in '65, to Hendrix, right up to the Chili Peppers at the Super Bowl and beyond. The most expensive guitars ever sold at auction were Stratocasters, and you think, this guitar is so special, and an American Fender guitar is the essence of this company. What I'm confessing to you is a very real and virtuous re-examination of the Fender brand, and an elevation within this company. This is an American product. There's a resurrection of

Justin Norvell: "As a Gen Xer, I approached products with a different lens. It's less about shredding and soloing and more about using the guitar as a sonic paintbrush."

Larry Thomas:
"We needed to open the factory for people to see. This is sacred ground."

pride manifested on the factory floor. The people who work here are less interested in Fenders made anywhere else. Inside the company, we never forget—*never* forget—this is a special place to work, and what we do is important to musicians. There is a resurrection of pride and esteem about what this brand is and how we are different from any other brand in the industry.

LT: For a time, our factory was closed to the public. We needed to open it for people to see. This is sacred ground. Let's show the workers the respect they deserve. Let's get their families and friends in there so they can see all this great work, and so kids can be proud of what their moms and dads are doing. Believe it or not, it was closed even to the Fender executives from Scottsdale who were charged with quality control.

So when I came in as CEO, I met the whole staff and said, okay, we are going to start traveling. Their budgets had been frozen, and our Scottsdale guys weren't traveling to the factory or to the dealers. I said, first thing, let's go to the Ontario [California] distribution center and look at the product sitting in the warehouse. We started there and worked backwards, examining everything and going to the factory to reconsider processes and materials. We hired some people to work under Sergio, and I rallied these new guys along with some workers in the factory to innovate. There's no reason why great ideas shouldn't be coming from there as well as from the product guys in Scottsdale.

RM: Transforming the entire company to attract new customers requires understanding the world we live in, which is extraordinarily fragmented. It is not a one-size-fits-all world. Personalization matters. Respecting unique needs is essential. It's not about trying to force a solution on our customers. It's about listening.

Justin Norvell: That's where social media comes in. It has altered marketing strategies across the industry. It's a sea change. You do have to wade through noise, but at the same time, we're closer to our customers than ever before, and we can pinpoint our target markets. With chat rooms, blogs, Facebook, and all the rest, it's a multi-voiced conversation now, with feedback going every which way—among ourselves, players, dealers, and media. There is no longer a one-way street where manufacturers communicate through catalogs. There are ways to send a message to all the people who are passionately devoted to vintage, for example, or we can fine-tune a marketing message to people of a certain age who might be on a budget.

Rather than trying to put the genie back into the bottle, we embrace these changes and recognize that, like everybody else, we can keep learning. We have something like one-and-a-half million people on our Facebook page. We can ask people what they think, and we listen. We

can reach people not only through our websites and chat rooms, but also through the artists' sites, the record companies' sites, fan clubs, biographies, and on and on. In the old days, if your local dealer decided not to buy a particular model, you might never know that it existed. But now, we can reach the people who would likely care about it, even if it's a relatively narrow sub-group.

RM: The next piece is innovation and technology. We have iOS Stratocasters, USB direct devices, ways of hooking up your guitar to the iPad, and we're working on things where you can record directly to the cloud as you play. We have to innovate, not just with product ideas but with process ideas as well.

LT: Price-wise, we needed bigger margins between the Mexican Fenders and the USA Fenders. Players buy with their eyes, and this guitar has just got to speak to you, so let's build some really pretty, exclusive, high-end instruments and not discount them, so we started building guitars with highly figured maple necks and beautiful rosewood. Chris Roberts had come to us from Gibson and now works for Breedlove [as production manager]. He introduced hand staining, so we started doing that. Somebody else took a guitar out to the parking lot one day and took a torch to it and got this really interesting effect. We tried sandblasting finishes to give it a rough look; we tried oil staining, all sorts of effects.

RM: Things like a compound-radius neck—only the Custom Shop could do that years ago, but we can do that in the factory now. We are not a little shop. We make more professional quality guitars than anybody on a global basis, and for an organization of our size to incorporate these luthier-type details into the factory is a major undertaking. It's a lot different than a *guy* learning the same things. Everything has to improve. You cannot stand still.

LT: We tried all sorts of ideas. We tried carved-top guitars with figured woods like they did at Gibson. We tried lightweight guitars, new paint colors, new neck designs like Channel Bound—that came from one of the engineers on the factory floor, and we put his name on the patent. We also tried reversing that, with a maple fingerboard inlaid into a solid rosewood neck. We experimented like crazy, even with distressed woods. We bought some old barns, got some old pine—some of this wood was 100 or 150 years old. Some pieces had knots or drill holes or nail holes. Another thing I wanted to do was to make the guitars more resonant, even when they weren't plugged in. I bought a scale and put it in the factory, and we started weighing the bodies. We experi-

Richard McDonald:
"The most important thing in the world to us is right on the factory floor in Southern California."

mented with chambering the bodies, and with stuffing the bodies, where you take out sections of wood and then replace them with other types of wood, just to see the effects on tone.

Another big change—we installed robots to do under-coating. The old way, if the guy happened to lean too far in, it put extra thickness in that spot. The robots really increased our first-pass approval. Stabilizing the undercoat with consistency makes it an easier job when it ends up in buffing. At the end of my third year, we reintroduced lacquer on lacquer, and that's one thing that separates the Pure Vintage series. They are as close to what Leo was building as the company has ever done. We do a lacquer sealer, a lacquer finish, and a lacquer clear coat. I put Mike Lewis on Pure Vintage because he is such a great details guy. I think vintage was something like a $10 million business for us the first year. It's been a great staple.

RM: With Pure Vintage, we're able to satisfy vintage guys better than ever. There's also been a lot of develop-ments in pickups over the past 10 years—like Samarium Cobalt pickups and the Noiseless technology in American Deluxes. We have new kinds of wiring, like solderless cir-cuits [see the American Deluxe Strat Plus]. Some of these things are directed to younger, fully digitized, tech-savvy customers. It's a challenge to matter to young bands and to fulfill the creative needs of young musicians when your brand is 60-plus years old, but that's a huge part of what we do. Artist relations are crucial, especially with emerg-ing, cutting-edge players. Some of these shredders are incredibly talented, but so much of this has already been done by Steve Vai, Joe Satriani, Eric Johnson, and Yngwie. Somebody has already done the double backflip on a motorcycle.

Take John Mayer, a genuine guitar guy. He's been extraordinarily influential as a Strat player over the last decade. For the people who are making a lot of new music, it's not always about the guitar player as a shred-der virtuoso. There are a lot of guys who were inspired by people like The Edge or bands like Coldplay. The guitar is about textures and creating a sonic landscape, and not so much about, hey, watch me shred. That's a big change, and Fender has appealed really well on both the guitar and amplifier level with that kind of artist. We are not just in the guitar business. We are in the music business, and our guitars and basses and amplifiers all have to evolve because music evolves. We can sustain product excellence because our designers and workers are so good. Sustaining continuing relevance is trickier.

JN: Our commitment to maintaining relevance is reflected in evolving not only our products but also our internal leadership. Think of the vision of Mike Lewis and Richard McDonald when they handed the baton over to me. Our stewardship of the brand includes keeping up with changes in our audiences in the modern spectrum, and as a Gen Xer, I approached products with a different lens than the guys who grew up with that echelon of guitar gods and classic virtuosos. John Mayer, Billy Corgan from Smash-ing Pumpkins, Jim Root from Slipknot, Jonny Buckland in Coldplay—guys like that were previously unrepresented in the product line and now find a place in the Fender family. New signature models reflect customers' evolving tastes and new approaches. It's less about shredding and soloing and more about using the guitar as a sonic paintbrush.

We all feel that we should innovate constantly. After all, Leo did.
– Larry Thomas

Timelessness

And the Sanctity of Golden Handcuffs

From an interview with Justin Norvell

A Stratocaster, as long as you keep its golden handcuffs on, can be all things to all people. Rock, heavy metal, country rock, country, funk, soul, blues, and pretty much every other style—there is no limit. By making all of our variations in the Stratocaster, we can keep its essential truth but tweak it to appeal to many different styles, ages, and genres.

So versatility is key, but at the same time, look at the Stratocaster's timelessness. How many other products look like their ancestors from 1954? What if you walked into a Chevrolet dealership and to the untrained eye the brand-new Chevy was almost indistinguishable from its 60-year-old predecessor? We just don't see that kind of thing across the spectrum of consumer goods, especially not in technological fields. Hammers and nails might not have changed much, but musical instruments is one field where we deal with a lot of guys who may play through complex effects racks, digital stompboxes, and advanced amplifier rigs and still want a traditional Stratocaster at the front end.

Now, what do we mean by golden handcuffs? We mean it in a positive way. It's not so much a limitation as it is a recognition that the Strat has a personality. It's something we all hold dear. There is a construct and an aesthetic that has to be maintained, or else it's not a Stratocaster anymore. It's something else. A Strat has to be a Strat, but within that we can offer a great deal of variety. People have different tastes and want their guitars to do different things, so it's a balance. Certain things are acceptable, and other things are blasphemy. We are very aware of drawing the balance properly. It's a great historical legacy that we inherited, something that we have to maintain and respect and continue. Look at things like the VG Strat, the iOS guitar, the TriplePlay, and so on. They tap into the latest technologies that mix software, computers, and iPads, but if you skip all that and just plug that guitar into a Princeton or a Twin, it's still a great, bone-simple Strat.

The way it feels is a big part of it. It's primal, intuitive. People want that Strat because it works, and because Leo Fender got it so right from the very beginning. We believe in its purity. Unlike a lot of instruments, the guitar is something you hold against your body. You feel it vibrating, resonating. It becomes a part of you. That young player today might not be familiar with Eric Clapton, let alone Buddy Holly. But the Strat continues to appeal, continues to work, continues to speak to the musician looking to express himself. This is not a Luddite perspective or necessarily even a vintage-purist kind of thing. It's simply a recognition that unlike almost all other mid-'50s designs, the Stratocaster has stood the test of time, even in a field of music that has seen revolutions come and go. That's the enduring quality of the Fender Stratocaster. It is a direct connection to your head and your heart.

The 50th Anniversary 1954 Stratocaster was one of the most ambitious projects ever undertaken by the Custom Shop. Master Builder Chris Fleming spearheaded the effort in 2004—the Strat's 50th year—working with George Blanda and their colleagues in marketing and R&D. Given the variations in original 1954 Stratocasters, a key decision was picking one guitar as a starting point. They selected Richard Smith's pristine '54, serial number 0100, which had also been scrutinized during the planning of the 40th Anniversary Strat a decade earlier. (Richard's guitar would be disassembled and inspected yet again during the Pure Vintage and 60th Anniversary projects; it was sold in 2014 for $250,000.)

The 50th Anniversary guitar was a benchmark in the Custom Shop's ever-increasing meticulousness in recreating the parts, specs, and processes of the company's golden age.

American Deluxe in Candy Apple Red
with a gold vinyl pickguard.

American Deluxe

Conceived as the top-of-the-line factory Strat, the American Deluxe debuted in 1998 and was revised in 2004 and again in 2010. Over the years, distinctive details have included several varieties of Noiseless pickups (Samarium Cobalts and N3s, e.g.), a roller nut (later dropped), staggered locking tuners, abalone dots, a Biflex neck rod, no-load tone controls (which are altogether bypassed when rotated all the way to 10), an extra fret (compared to vintage spec), a beveled heel, and a 2-point trem with a pop-in arm.

Fender's ingenious S-1 switching system was introduced in the summer of 2003 and has appeared on several Fender instruments, including American Deluxe Strats. It's perfect for Strat players who want more tonal versatility but don't want to spoil the guitar's traditional look with extra knobs or switches. The center of the stock-looking volume knob is a barely noticeable push switch that when indented activates the S-1. Over the years the system has been reconfigured several times, typically offering the introduction of a special capacitor into the circuit, previously unattainable pickup combinations, variations in series vs. parallel connection, in-phase vs. out-of-phase wiring, and a reassignment of the knobs' functions.

In yet another example of how one Fender project impacts others, development of the Eric Johnson model was in some ways a turning point in the American Deluxe's 2010 redesign, as was the case regarding the American Standard's revision a year or two earlier. Justin Norvell: "We went so deep into what makes a guitar sound good, and we had to free our minds from accepted wisdom in some cases. People would say, well, we have to make these pickups out of alnico 5 and so on, but with the American Deluxe, instead of having a set of identical pickups, we ended up doing an alnico 5 in the bridge, where it's a little hotter; an alnico 3 in the neck, where it's a little rounder; and an alnico 2 in the middle, which sounds really sweet. The approach was to voice the pickup specifically for each position under the string." The 2010 upgrade also entailed a compound-radius fingerboard—9.5" to 14"—a comfortable and practical detail previously exclusive to Custom Shop Fenders.

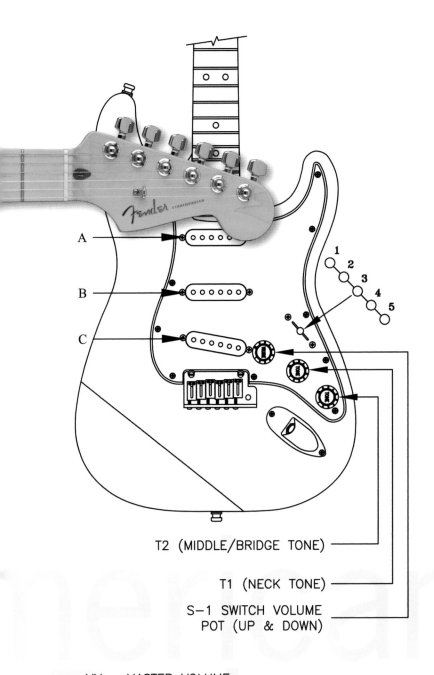

A

B

C

T2 (MIDDLE/BRIDGE TONE)

T1 (NECK TONE)

S-1 SWITCH VOLUME
POT (UP & DOWN)

MV = MASTER VOLUME
T1 = NECK TONE
T2 = MID/BRIDGE TONE
+ = SERIES CONNECTION
/ = PARALLEL CONNECTION
SC = SPECIALS CAPACITOR

5 WAY SW POSITIONS, S-1 SWITCH UP

1	2	3	4	5	POSITION
MV T1	MV T1+T2	MV T2	MV T2	MV T2	CONTROL
●	●	○	○	○	← NECK (A)
○	●	●	●	○	← MIDDLE (B)
○	○	○	●	●	← BRIDGE (C)
	A/B		B/C		CONNECTION

5 WAY SW POSITIONS, S-1 SWITCH DOWN

1	2	3	4	5	POSITION
MV T1	MV T1+T2	MV T2	MV T2	MV T2	CONTROL
●	●	●	○	○	← NECK (A)
●	●	●	●	●	← MIDDLE (B)
○	○	●	●	●	← BRIDGE (C)
A+B	(A/SC) + B	(A/C) + B	B + (C/SC)	B+C	CONNECTION

●	PICKUP IS ON
○	PICKUP IS OFF
A	PICKUP (NECK)
B	PICKUP (MIDDLE)
C	PICKUP (BRIDGE)

The American Deluxe's array of controls has evolved over the years, but this diagram provides a typical example of the guitar's sonic flexibility.

Is solder outdated? Fender thinks so. Richard McDonald: "Solder is a thing of the past. It's unpredictable, not particularly roadworthy. Fenders have always been easy to modify, to customize, but now, on a guitar like the Strat Plus, if you want to reconfigure the controls and functions, you can just pop in one of our little interchangeable 'personality cards.' It takes about 15 seconds."

These passive, no-battery-needed cards are made possible by advances in surface-mounted PC board technologies that entail ever-smaller capacitors, resistors, and other components. Each card reroutes the signal path in a specific way. You could have multiple volume controls, an added treble bleed, different tone-circuit signal paths, pickup-blending options, and more. The eminently practical American Deluxe Strat Plus HSS, introduced in 2014, also features locking tuners and a compound-radius fingerboard.

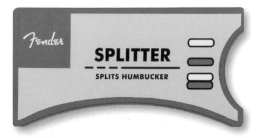

A plug-in hybrid of a different sort, the American Deluxe Strat Plus offers multiple, quick-change personalities.

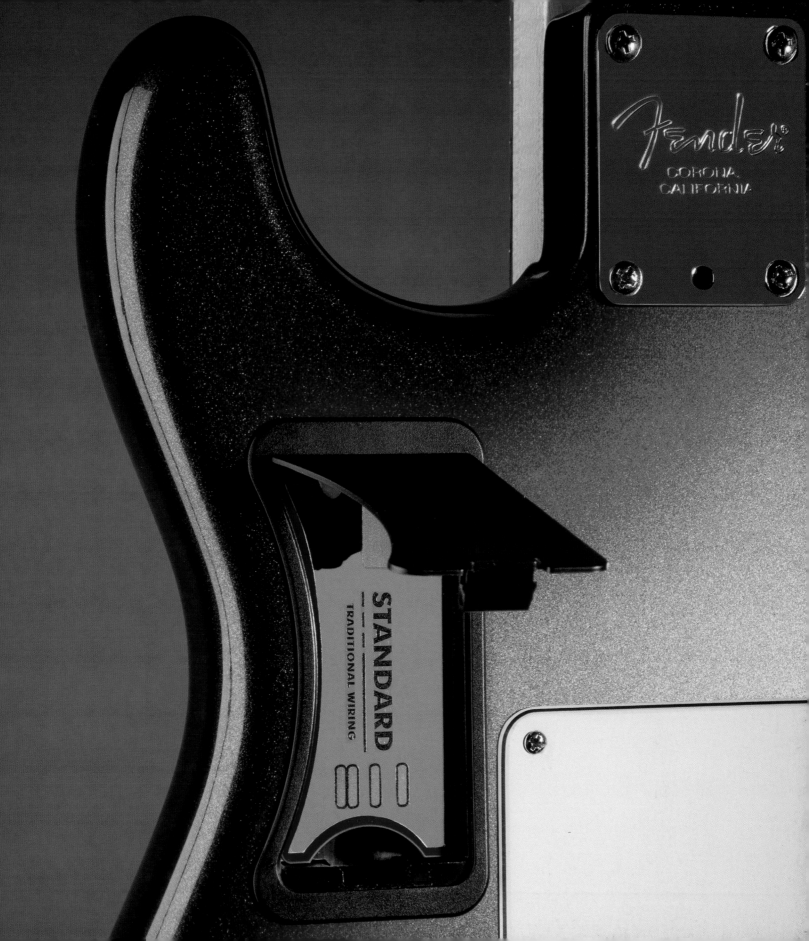

American Standard, HSS version in Blizzard Pearl.

Return to Form
Revising the American Standard

Shortly after William Schultz and his associates acquired Fender from CBS in 1985, Dan Smith and George Blanda took on a daunting challenge: Build a better Stratocaster. As explained in the original edition of this book: "Not a reissue, not a cost-cutter, not a 'Cadillac,' not an import—just a basic U.S. Strat." If they had any "advantage" at all, it was a widespread recognition that the Strats of the '70s and early '80s could indeed use some improvement. The Strats of the early and mid 2000s, however, were hardly perceived as fixer-uppers, at least in the minds of most players. Nevertheless, in 2008 VP Justin Norvell and his colleagues decided that updates—well, not just updates; improvements, actually—were required. They drew from Master Builder Chris Fleming's experience in crafting the 50th Anniversary Custom Shop 1954 reissue, by all accounts one of the best Strats ever.

Ritchie Fliegler was one of Fender's most significant senior executives of the past several decades. (When he headed up the amplifier department, he not only completely restructured the line but also taught Fender amp designers and marketers how to listen, how to hear subtleties they had been missing. Eventually, Marketing Services, Advertising, Artist Relations, Licensed Goods and Accessories, and all of the individual Fender product marketing/development heads reported to him, although at the time of the following story, he had moved on to other responsibilities at Fender.) Justin Norvell: "Ritchie is very discerning, a tough customer to please. He loves Chris Fleming's Anniversary '54, and there was kind of a seamless segue from that guitar to the American Standard redo of 2008. Ritchie took me into the sound room and said, 'Why does this guitar sound so good? It's perfect!' This sparked a series of discussions about the recipe. It was very deep. I would wake up in the middle of the night thinking about it."

Ritchie had acquired his '54 reissue from then-CEO Bill Schultz. Schultz had asked Ritchie and Mark Kendrick to catalog his personal collection, which included among other things the first production sample of every guitar introduced during his tenure. Ritchie Fliegler: "The project is over and Bill calls me in to his office, still piled high with all the cases. 'Thanks for the great job, take one.' 'Um, er ...' 'I said take one! Before I change my mind!'" Ritchie picked the Chris Fleming Strat (its serial number informally referred to as "minus 1"), from an official series of 50 (51, including the Schultz/Fliegler guitar). One day, Ritchie's band, the Saucy Jacks, was preparing to rehearse for their debut at a Fender Band Jam. "I wandered around the building looking for a regular guitar," he remembers. "No matter where I looked, with guitars on every wall and in every nook, there was nothing that wasn't some 'improved' version of perfection. I went to [Richard] McDonald and asked, 'Do we make just a regular Strat or Tele any more? You know—regular bridge, plain pickups, no silly tone controls, a radiused fingerboard, etc.? You know—a Strat?' 'No, that would have to be special-ordered from the Custom Shop.' I went mental. Really? I had to bring my own guitar to a jam—at Fender? So I grabbed the Bill Schultz/Fleming Strat from home."

Another discussion addressed how hot the lead pickup needed to be on a mainstream, factory Fender. Ritchie Fliegler: "Over the years, there was a continual 'heating up' process in response to field comments that the pickups, especially the lead position, were weak. Based on my experience with older instruments, and now with the brand-new Fleming guitar in my hands (all of which had pickups much less hot than the contemporaneous stuff), I could show that this was a mechanical problem, not a pickup problem." Ritchie explains that as a mechanical system, if the guitar itself—strings, wood, hardware, etc.—generates a weak, low-energy signal to begin with, the pickups cannot take up the slack. "The reason each instrument sounds different is that each instrument *is* different," he points out. "How string energy is transmitted to the body, what is lost or affected along the way, is also a big part. That is why a Les Paul with a stop bar sounds totally different from one with a Tune-o-matic, even if it's the same guitar modified in that way."

Previous factory alterations to Stratocasters had included the "swimming pool" rout under the pickguard, which provided a generic, one-size-fits-all production convenience; it also removed a lot of wood. Changes had also been made to other details. "The Strat had become a very 'lossy' mechanical system," Ritchie explains, referring to the loss of string energy caused by production shortcomings. "Pickups could not pick up the slack if they weren't 'seeing' a 'fat' waveform in

American Standard, Sienna Sunburst.

the first place—there was no fat signal to enhance, no information to grab."

After his encounter with Ritchie Fliegler, Justin Norvell had his R&D colleagues build a set of Stratocasters for testing purposes. Each guitar was intended to enable designers to focus on one fine detail or another—the composition of the bridge saddles, for example. To provide meaningful comparisons of these isolated aspects, the test guitars were otherwise as identical as was humanly possible to build, their equally weighted bodies crafted from the same wood stock, their finishes precisely measured to the same thickness, and so on. Months of testing followed.

Justin Norvell: "It was time to pare it back down, to look at the entire set of ingredients all over again. I came to think it's like writing a song: If you layer too many things on top of it, you are in danger of losing the essence. What is the essence of the Stratocaster? Part of this journey was taking previous opinions and 60 years of folklore out of the equation, so we were doing double-blind tests with large groups of players. It resulted in the reintroduction of the American Standard in 2008, just tweaking the tiniest parts of the recipe. It's like the master chef who knows that sometimes a dash of sugar in a recipe that's not sweet can be the final flourish. We kept open minds to any and all possibilities and took nothing for granted. For example, we went through a dozen different body woods. For saddles, we went back to the vintage-style, bent-steel type with narrower spacing. We changed the bridge block, and went to a thinner finish with less of an undercoat. We also put a bit of gloss back on the neck. The necks had been satined out since 1986—bone white with no gloss, more of that Charvel-style finish—and we went back to having a bit more of a tint, a little less '80s-ish.

"One of the things Eric Johnson said when we did his signature Stratocaster is that small things can make a huge difference, and he's right. We did make the American Standard look a little more traditional, but every change was made for reasons of performance, not style or looks, and this return to form went over extremely well, with a very positive trajectory in the marketplace. We are always pushing for innovation, but sometimes, when you come back to the core, that recipe is intact and true, and it always resonates."

Brownie
and Other Assorted Love Songs

Eric Clapton bought his first Stratocaster, a well-worn '56, on May 7, 1967. He nicknamed it Brownie and played it on one of the most exalted albums of the entire rock era: 1970's *Layla and Other Assorted Love Songs*. The maple-neck, two-color sunburst Strat, serial no. 12073, is currently on display at the Experience Music Project museum in Seattle.

The Custom Shop accepted the task of duplicating the guitar as a Tribute model. Having spearheaded the supremely successful Blackie project and having personally built numerous guitars for Eric Clapton, Todd Krause was the logical choice to direct the Brownie project (although he modestly suggests, "Any of the Master Builders could have done it"). The Tribute of 2013 has all the features one would expect of a '56 clone—a maple neck with a 7.25" radius and vintage-style frets, single-ply pickguard, nitro lacquer, etc.—but it also bears meticulous recreations of the nicks, dings, scratches, dents and cigarette burns on Clapton's historic guitar.

On the earlier Blackie project, once Krause's prototype had been approved, each of the Master Builders crafted a set of Tributes. This time around, however, Todd built all 100. It took the better part of a year. Todd Krause: "It might have seemed to the public that it took a couple of months, but I had been working on it in secret for months and months before word got out. We had learned a lot doing Blackie, and this time around the process was smoother. I simply had more time, less of a rush.

"With a guitar like that, there is a lot of history involved. It's an honor to hold it and play it and keep it for a while, and a little scary. Every little thing has a story behind it, so you can't help but get a sense of the man and his music, all the performances and recordings. Every little detail is almost a puzzle. In the tremolo cavity, for example, there was this real interesting chip where part of the body had broken off, either when the guitar was originally routed, or maybe somebody put a screwdriver in there to pry out a spring or something. At first I was a little worried about how I was going to go about doing that detail on each guitar, but it worked out pretty cool. So there's always a whole list of these sorts of things."

Brownie sports five springs, no cover plate, and "buckle rash" similar to that of the Custom Shop's other Clapton Strat clone, Blackie (pp. 96-97).

Todd inspected and measured Brownie in Seattle, and halfway through the project he checked it again to gauge his progress to date. On a third occasion, the finished proto was compared to the original side by side. Todd says, "One of the lessons I learned from Blackie was that I wanted to do my own inspection of the finished prototype right alongside the original, rather than just sending it to EMP and getting a list of things they thought should be changed. Seeing the two side by side was actually a little weird. That's how close they were.

"In some ways it struck me as amazing that Blackie and Brownie were so similar. You can explain it; after all, the same person played both Strats for many years. But some similarities really stood out. If you look at the backs, Eric has the trem cover removed and there's the same sort of heavy buckle rash. Opening it up, the electronics have been reworked in a similar fashion, with the shielded cavity.

"Blackie was amazing, but if anything I liked Brownie even better. Blackie's neck was undersized because it had been refinished, but Brownie was an earlier '56, so they hadn't transitioned away from that fatter shape yet. The neck is chunky and feels really, really good. The whole guitar feels really, really good."

Back in Black
David Gilmour's 6-String Lab Experiment

Scores of books have been written about individual guitar brands, and a growing number of volumes, including this one, address a single model. But an entire book devoted to a single guitar? That distinction belongs to *Pink Floyd: The Black Strat—A History of David Gilmour's Black Fender Stratocaster*, written by Gilmour's personal guitar tech of four decades, Phil Taylor.

Gilmour's Fender was already a bit unusual when he bought it in the late spring of 1970, in that it featured a somewhat rare maple-cap fingerboard. Otherwise, it was a fairly typical late-'60s CBS guitar, but not for long. Over the next several decades it would be modified constantly and drastically, as David used it for classic solos on Pink Floyd's *Dark Side of the Moon*, *Wish You Were Here*, *The Wall*, and more. As explained in *The Dream Factory: Fender Custom Shop*, "The guitar became not only David's instrument of choice for many years, but also a mobile experimental lab of sorts." Its pickguard, volume knob, neck, neck plate, and tremolo were all replaced, some several times. David tried 21- and 22-fret necks, maple and rosewood fingerboards, humbuckers and single-coils, stock string nuts and locking units, stock and custom wirings, and standard and dropped-D tunings. Its half-dozen necks were fitted with at least four brands of tuners.

Various switches were installed, then removed, then re-installed; the wiring was tweaked and re-tweaked.

Pickups were replaced. While the Strat's basic construction has always lent itself to component replacement, the level of modification on this guitar went much further than swapping out pickups or tuners. Routs were dug, sometimes rather crudely. Holes were drilled, then filled. It's likely that no guitar on earth has undergone so many field-hospital surgeries or sported so many distinct personalities as the Black Strat.

In the fall of 2006, the Custom Shop's Mike Eldred and Todd Krause met with Phil Taylor to initiate discussions of a Custom Shop re-creation of this most unusual of Fenders. Debates ensued. Taylor insisted on re-creating many of the instrument's quirks—a costly proposition—while Gilmour himself wanted the model to be relatively affordable. Various balances and compromises were drawn, and finally, after years of planning and negotiating, the Custom Shop introduced Relic and NOS versions of the Custom Artist Series David Gilmour Stratocaster. The balance was drawn this way: The shop duplicated the player-oriented details, including neck shape, an extra toggle switch/pickup selector, the stubby little trem bar (which is comfy and practical, by the way), and the vintage-spec fingerboard radius. Todd Krause: "The Relic version looks a lot like David's guitar, but we didn't do the maniacal level of detail you see on a Tribute, where we duplicate every microscopic scratch and ding."

Black

The Gilmour's extra toggle is the tiny chrome dot between the first two knobs, just to the right.

Master Design in Green and Gold

Eldred to Krause: Build your dream guitar. Not the one you think will sell well, but the one you would make for yourself, right now. Todd Krause: "I had already started on it. This was going to be my personal guitar. I was going to take my tax return and buy it [laughs]. When he gave me this assignment, I was about three quarters of the way done. A week later, he had a guitar in his hands."

Krause was influenced by his work on the Brownie project. Although he installed Fat '50s on his Master Design Strat, the cavity is shielded, Brownie-style. "It changes the tone," he says, "and it's very cool, a classic rock sound." The 5-way switch and knobs operate conventionally, but a treble-bleed resistor on the volume knob keeps the tone from changing so dramatically when the volume is backed off. Todd liked the way Brownie's plastic parts had aged at different rates, providing a contrast in color. "I've always liked that look," he says, "especially on a '60s guitar with the white/black/white pickguard and aged yellow covers. The Brownie was like that, although some of these things don't show up in photographs. You don't see them until you hold it in your hands."

Todd managed to come up with a new color that would have fit right in with the vintage automotive paints Leo Fender adapted in the 1950s and 1960s. "It looks like it could have come from a Ford Country Squire wagon with the wood panels on the side," Todd says. "Normally, I don't use gold hardware if it's up to me. But on that guitar, I couldn't *not* do it. The green just really wanted the gold. The parts are reliced but not rusted, so the gold shows up more. Think of the hardware as a particularly heavy Closet Classic. Also, I didn't remove a lot of paint from the body. I wanted the player to have his influence on the look just by playing it for a long time."

Todd's favorite neck is also the favorite among Custom Shop customers, the 10/56. Patterned after a neck dated October 1956—hence 10/56—it's a relatively big V neck, of the type often called "boatneck" (although such terms aren't always consistently applied). While his Master Design Strat has a strong vintage vibe, the truss rod is the non-vintage, headstock-adjust type. Todd reports that players often ask about necks that move around a bit. He knows all about it. In Corona, California, home to the Custom Shop, the humidity can go from 100 percent to zero overnight, so a bit of neck bowing or back-bowing is to be expected. Todd Krause: "If it's raining outside, I will check the tuner and the notes are slightly flat. That's natural at miniscule levels. But some people take the tension off the strings to put the guitar in the case. Don't do that. It's a balance, and if you keep detuning your guitar, you're asking for trouble. Even though the Master Design has a 10/56 neck, I made it headstock-adjust, which makes it a lot easier. When musicians are moving around and encountering different humidities, or they're on the road and the guitars are being jostled, why not make it convenient?"

At this point it would be difficult for Todd Krause to design his dream guitar; he's already done it. Perhaps in a few years, new experiences or changing tastes might inspire a new direction. "But right now," he says, "this is the guitar for me. If people like it, they can get the Master Design, but it's limited to 2014."

The limited-production concept has been a cornerstone of the Custom Shop's marketing approach during the past decade, and it's proved effective. Mike Eldred: "It creates an urgency when you're offering only 50 guitars, or maybe even as few as 10 guitars of a certain color, or you are offering them for only one year, or even a single quarter, like the 1st Quarter Stratocaster. It creates excitement." Mike reports that when dealers are informed that guitars they want are no longer available, they sometimes sign up for the next round of limited models without knowing what they will be, a remarkable leap of faith in any business. "It's what happens in the auto industry," Mike says, "like when Ferrari announces an upcoming, super-limited model and then they are all pre-sold. That's a very good thing. I took some of these philosophies from car companies and watch companies that do that sort of thing."

Michael Landau Signature Relic

The two Michael Landau Artist Collection Signature Relic Stratocasters provide a good example of the lengths to which the Custom Shop will go to please a valued artist. Mike Eldred: "It takes a long time to build a real rapport with an artist, a relationship that's not just a flash in the pan. I pursued my goal with Michael for probably 10 years or so. He was like, *no, no, no, no*–but finally, I made a guitar and went over to his house and took a few pictures. I said, let's do an ad, and put a picture of your new album in the ad and help sell some records. And he goes, you'd do that for me? I said, yeah, no strings attached. He couldn't believe it. So it started as a project that I slipped under the radar, and it turned into a signature guitar. These are the kinds of things that typically don't get done in big companies, but doing stuff like that builds trust with an artist."

As we go to press, the shop offers two Relic versions of the Landau Strat, a '63 and a '68. Except for their headstocks, colors, and fretboard dots, they are identical. Both feature pickups based on a set of Fat '50s, although normally the middle pickup would be a reverse wound/

reverse polarity unit, but on the Landaus, all three pickups are wound and polarized in the same direction. Master Builder Jason Smith built three prototypes and worked with the artist in bringing the project to fruition. He reports: "His [original] '63 has his favorite neck shape, and it's pretty odd. It's not a normal C shape. It has slightly offset shaping in back, with a lot of shoulder on the bass side up to the 5th fret; above that, it flip-flops, with more shoulder on the treble side. It was unusual, and it had been refretted, but the shape was totally stock and unmodified; that was just how the factory guy happened to sand it that day."

Connoisseurs of sunburst finishes may note that the 3-color burst on the Landau Strat is particularly beautiful. Jason Smith calls it a bleached burst. "They had a great finish in '68 because they bleached the wood. It lightens the color of the alder, so when you spray the yellow and red it's a lot more vibrant." The Signature models have been reliced to match Landau's personal guitars.

C'est Chic
Nile Rodgers' Hitmaker

As the cofounder and guitarist of Chic, Nile Rodgers created irresistibly catchy riffs that established him as a world-class funkmeister—and yet there's so much more to his talent and vision. As a guitarist, producer, composer, and arranger, he has contributed to albums selling more than a staggering 100 million copies. He's worked with David Bowie, Diana Ross, David Lee Roth, Debbie Harry, Duran Duran, and Daft Punk—and those are just the Ds. Robert Plant, Jeff Beck, Stevie Ray and Jimmie

Vaughan, Mick Jagger, Steve Winwood, Michael Jackson, Madonna—Rodgers' resume is notable not only for its length but also for the artistry and star power of his collaborators. It's no wonder his well-worn hardtail Stratocaster is nicknamed the Hitmaker.

The Custom Shop collaborated with Nile Rodgers on a limited-edition, Tribute-series recreation of his lightweight, much-recorded guitar. Some of the measurements were taken at Nile's home in New York, and the work was completed in the Corona shop. Master Builder Paul Waller initially focused on the pickups, later inherited the entire project, and ultimately discovered that the Hitmaker's departures from stock specs—in body depth, pickguard, nut width, neck shape, fingerboard, and knobs—made it a bit of *le freak*.

Waller started with 1959 Stratocaster specs (the Hitmaker has one of the original-spec, one-piece maple necks that Fender was using up as it transitioned into the mid-'59 rosewood boards). As Paul got deeper into the project, he realized that the body was about 50/1000ths of an inch thinner than usual, front to back. "When you look at enough Strats, you can tell," he says. "It's a noticeable discrepancy, and that might have been why it was made into a hardtail. Otherwise, a tremolo bridge block might have poked out the back and scraped the cover plate."

Waller prepared three pickguard/pickup assemblies and sent them to Nile. "He's a savvy guy," Paul says.

The Hitmaker's factory finish was sunburst, but Nile's admiration of Jimi Hendrix led him to have the guitar refinished in Olympic White. "Or maybe he did it himself," Paul says, "but in any case it was a professional job. It looked factory." The refin was hardly the last of the many departures from original specs. "I found that the neck was tremendously undersized," Paul recounts, "oversanded at the factory and very thin from front to back, with really asymmetrical shaping in back; it's lopsided but not in a bad way. There is a little bit more shoulder on one side of the neck, but in a different area there's more shoulder on the other side, with a taper from one to the other. There's also extra wear around the 7th fret; Nile has spent a *lot* of time there—that's his zone. It required changing our tooling a bit to get the truss rod to sit a little closer to the frets so we could back-shape the neck and not worry about the truss rod poking

"He used to do repairs in New York and knows his way around a guitar. He wired the assemblies into the Hitmaker himself. It was like the three bears—one set of pickups was a little hotter, one was a little colder, and one was in the middle. He picked the middle set, and those matched the readings we took on his originals. He told us he couldn't tell the difference in sound, and of course that's what we were looking for."

Arrangements were made for Nile to send his guitar to the shop. Apparently, he always uses a gig bag and didn't have a case, so they sent him a hardshell G&G case for shipping, and that's how it arrived in Corona—no box, just a guitar case wrapped in gaffer's tape with the label stuck right to the Tolex. Paul Waller: "I took a picture and sent it to Mike Eldred, and he said, *you gotta be kidding me!* Nile's most prized possession on the planet, and that's how he shipped it [laughs]. But the guitar was fine."

through the back.

"The fingerboard edges are heavily rolled, and the nut is also a little undersized. Originally, I did not think to measure that part of the neck, but Nile played an early sample and he is so in tune with his guitar that he could tell the difference right away. I measured it, and sure enough, he was right; it was off just a bit. It's no wonder he could never find another Strat like his. He owns several, but the Hitmaker has these aberrations, and we replicated all those things on the Tribute." Other details: a chrome-plated brass pickguard, a 9.5" radius (like Nile's guitar, which had been refretted), Sperzel tuners, and speed knobs. Paul Waller reports that the Tribute Hitmaker has impressed players and dealers alike. As we go to press, the shop hasn't even finished building the 100-piece series, and all remaining guitars are pre-sold.

Awakening
The Pure Vintage Project

It's been decades since "pre-CBS" and "tweed" and "hardtail" were added to the lexicon. The generation who remembers Les Paul as a gifted artist and not just a Gibson solidbody have teenage or college-age kids of their own. Or grandchildren. Plenty of Generation Xers are in their 30s or 40s. Some are pushing 50. They didn't grow up on Buddy Holly or James Burton. Does vintage still matter?

Mike Lewis, VP of Product Marketing: "Yes. Older guys, collectors, and experienced players gravitate to authentic vintage reissues right away. The younger players grow into it. There's a big 'S curve' with that type of product. Same with things like tweed Bassmans. You get an early surge on them, then it levels off, and then it slowly comes back up with a spike again as people grow into it and discover it for themselves. You get a kid who starts off in punk or rap or death metal, and then they discover Stevie Ray Vaughan and go, wow, where has this guy been my whole life? And then they start simplifying and getting more roots-oriented. When I had my retail store, I saw this all the time. I would sell a kid an Ibanez and a Crate amplifier, and 10 years later he's playing a '62 Strat reissue and a '59 Bassman."

When Fender revised its American Vintage line in mid 2012, now grouping the instruments under the Pure Vintage label, a reasonable response might've been, well, we've seen this before, haven't we? Fender has been reissuing vintage-era Stratocasters since the early 1980s, beginning with the much-heralded '57 and '62 models under the direction of Dan Smith. Every time they do this, they tout the new models' ever-increasing authenticity. In terms of scrutinizing original instruments and duplicating specs as closely as humanly possible, what could they do this time around that they hadn't been doing for three decades?

Quite a lot, as it turns out. Far from a mere marketing campaign, the reimagining of the American Vintage line was a major undertaking for Fender and a highlight of Mike Lewis' long career. He explains: "Any time you undertake this sort of project, you do what you can, when you can do it, with the resources and tooling available at the time. If those resources evolve, then the guitars' authenticity can evolve as well." Former CEO Larry Thomas has an extensive collection, including some exceptional Strats. Richard McDonald, a fine player himself, spent time with these guitars and realized that some details—an ever-so-subtle richness in tone, a warmer feel, an extra grace in the vibe—had remained elusive despite Fender's several reissue programs. He returned to the factory on a mission: Revisit the reissues.

Fender picked Stratocasters that hadn't previously been recreated in the main factory. The selection of 1956, 1959, and 1965 was anything but random. Those three years account for four significant Stratocaster versions matching a variety of player preferences: big maple neck, '56; slimmer maple neck, early '59; slimmer neck/rosewood board, later '59; bigger neck/rosewood, '65. Michael Frank-Braun designed unique pickups for each model to match the specs and sounds of its respective year. Mike Lewis: "Also, by picking years that we hadn't done before, no one who had one of our previous American Vintage guitars would feel, hey, what about my guitar?"

George Blanda and Mike Lewis traveled around the country, visiting various dealers and collectors and spending days going through all-original vintage Stratocasters. "This was a new level of inspection," says Mike. "We were working at a forensic-autopsy level [laughs]. The necks came off, the pickguards came off, and we measured everything. I mean *everything*—every nook and cranny, every radius, every corner, every curve, every everything. We documented all the features, all the details."

One thing that helped Mike and his team to make the Pure Vintage guitars the factory's most authentic reissues ever was that they were careful to note both consistencies and inconsistencies among the originals. No one who knows anything about vintage Fenders will tell you that all Strats coming off the line in any given year (or any given *day*) were identical. They varied in all sorts of specs, sometimes rather surprisingly. Mike Lewis: "On the specs that were consistent, we duplicated them. When the specs were inconsistent, we went with the more common one, or simply the one we thought was the coolest. George and I are both players. We could pick up these guitars and make an assessment about what's going to be most practical for

"If resources evolve, authenticity can evolve as well."
— Mike Lewis

the player. When we went with the most player-centric option, it still had to be one hundred percent vintage-correct." Lewis estimates that "autopsies" were performed on about two dozen all-original pieces.

Back at the factory, body perimeters were redrawn from scratch, and designers began retooling bodies, routs, necks, headstocks, volutes, heels, neck pockets, holes for the tuners, and more. One important detail was the way the fingerboard edges "roll over." Mike Lewis: "Some processes are not always the most efficient from a manufacturing standpoint, but sometimes you have to duplicate the original process if you want to get it right. A great example is the way the neck rolls over. On most guitars, the neck curves from the back up to the edge of the fingerboard; the radius stops and the fingerboard starts. But on these guitars, that contour of the neck comes up alongside and continues to radius before joining the fingerboard. It's a feel thing. The first inclination might be to take knives and just

scrape those edges and roll it over that way, but you don't get the right effect. It has to be part of the original design, like the way they were cut in the first place on the originals. That little detail turns out to make a noticeable difference, not only in authenticity but in comfort. I think the necks and their rolled edges might be the most unique things about these Pure Vintage guitars."

Richard McDonald: "What we had previously been producing as an American Vintage guitar was already a high-quality homage to the work the company had done 40 or 50 years prior. But what we did with Pure Vintage wasn't just an investigation of guitars. It was an investigation of ourselves, our facilities, and our engineering. We actually recreated the work processes from way back, and these guitars turned out to be authentically unbelievable. It has

Mike Lewis with a slab-board American Vintage '59 Strat in faded Sonic Blue.

to be more than just being right with a caliper. It has to be right with the manufacturing sensibility. It's not only about how the guitar looks in the final stages, but also, how did we get there? Revising the American Vintage guitars turned into a journey for this entire company."

No matter how much we may revere all things vintage, modern machinery has made a huge leap forward when it comes to production consistency. Once the ideal specs are nailed, they can be replicated with a uniformity unknown to the old shop in Fullerton. Richard McDonald: "Even with all the benefits that we have today with CNC [computer numeric controlled] manufacturing, there is still something like 108 processes that we do by hand on every Stratocaster, not just a vintage model. But once we have worked so hard to uncover what is so special and cool about these guitars, the technology has given us the ability to reproduce that with consistency and reliability. If you played many vintage guitars, let's face it, sometimes the folklore is more awesome than the guitar [laughs]. Before we do all of the handwork, the factory craftspeople are starting with a core basic product that's been spec'd in a way that is much more refined and consistent than it ever was. We have a repeatability of all the details we value so highly."

For previous reissue projects, why hadn't Fender reproduced the old *FENDER PAT.PEND* bridge saddles? Lewis explains that the original tool had been worn out for years. "The original parts had a Metropolis/Art Deco vibe and looked crisp because that tool was once sharp and clean and perfect. Same thing with the string trees, so we invested in rebuilding the tools to get those details right on all four of the Pure Vintage Stratocasters." One inconsistency was the depth of the holes in the trem block where the strings attach. Lewis: "They must have hand-drilled those things, but the longer the string, the better the tone, so we measured that and selected the ideal spec."

One flaw in many of the much-maligned Fenders of the 1970s was a finishing process that cut costs but cut corners, too, smothering the guitar with a thick layer of polyester goop. It's hard to measure precisely what effect this might have had—given other production shortcomings—but there's no question that thin nitrocellulose finishes are favored for their ability to let a guitar breathe rather than suffocating any natural resonance it might have. The Pure Vintage Strats are "flash-coated," receiving a thin top coat of quickly applied nitro lacquer intended to contribute to vintage tone and appearance. Final details include string nuts made of genuine bone. Mike Lewis: "Many of the original guitars we looked at had bone nuts. The sound is more 'lively'—subtle, but noticeable. It was interesting that on most of the '50s instruments we examined, it looked like the same person had filed the nut slots."

The release of the new series was greeted with a chorus of rave reviews. Even the factory workers' colleagues over in the Custom Shop were impressed. Master Builder Greg Fessler: "Mike Lewis did such a fantastic job on the Pure Vintage that I think he matched anything we were doing over here. For a long time the role of the Custom Shop was to help train factory workers and improve their products, and   that is still true, but it goes both ways. With things like Pure Vintage, the factory guitars impressed everybody, including us. They really made us perk up and take notice, and we've used some of their advancements to improve our own vintage-spec guitars."

Guitar Player magazine's assessment of the rosewood-board '59 was typical: "The faded Sonic Blue color is gorgeous, the body is light, the mid-'60s C-shape neck feels wonderful, and the luxuriously dark rosewood fretboard is silky smooth." While early sales of the Pure Vintage line exceeded expectations, the project had ramifications beyond commercial success. Richard McDonald: "We rediscovered our past in a very significant way. It was an awakening."

"I tried one of those Pure Vintage guitars and was very pleasantly surprised. These new reissues are the best ones I've tried, in particular the pickups. They are just much more present and musical. There's definitely something there; you can tell as soon as you pick it up."

— Eric Johnson

"It wasn't just an investigation of guitars. It was an investigation of ourselves."

— Richard McDonald

Page 38: 1956, Shell Pink
Page 40: 1965, Shoreline Gold
Above: late 1959, Sherwood Green Metallic
1965, Dakota Red
early 1959, 3-color sunburst

Six Decades, Seven Guitars
An Anniversary Bash for the Ages

Introduction

Fender wasn't about to let the Stratocaster's 60th birthday pass by without "ballyhooing it to the skies," as Don Randall might have said in 1954. Ballyhoo is all well and good, but in this case, the considerable savvy of Fender marketers reflected rather than overshadowed the real-world production finesse of the factory and the Custom Shop.

The 2014 array of Anniversary Strats offered something for aficionados of every stripe and budget, from a Squier import to a Custom Shop Heavy Relic costing 10 or 12 times as much. A few less official, limited runs from the Custom Shop also joined the celebration. No fewer than six guitars were cataloged as Anniversary items from the factory. Fender helpfully arranged them in three categories—Past (American Vintage 1954), Present (60th Anniversary Commemorative, 60th Anniversary Classic Player '50s, and Squier 60th Anniversary Classic Vibe '50s) and Future (TriplePlay HSS, and Deluxe HSS Plus Top With iOS Connectivity)—although even the "Strats of the future" still reflected the restless creativity and mechanical ingenuity of Leo Fender's mind, circa 1953. Richard McDonald: "The 60th Anniversary Stratocasters are huge sellers. There is a global awareness of these products."

American Vintage '54

The 60th Anniversary American Vintage 1954 Stratocaster is limited in its 1,954-piece production and also in its 2014-only availability. At a list price of $2,500, it retails for 10 times the cost of its original forebear. (The comparison shows how expensive, not how cheap, the original was, given calculations for inflation. A $250 guitar was a major investment at a time when you could buy a showroom-shiny Chevy Bel Air for two grand.) It offers the expected deep-cut, 2-piece ash body, 2-color burst, a fingerboard with rolled edges and a 7.25" radius, vintage frets and vintage tremolo. Mike Lewis: "Chris Fleming and I spent many hours with original, unmodified 1954 Strats, and the pickups for the American Vintage Anniversary '54 were newly designed from scratch to duplicate the originals." An extra measure of authenticity is seen in the flash-coat lacquer finish, PAT.PEND. saddles, a bone nut, a round string tree, a walnut teardrop rod adjustment, and pickup covers and short-skirt knobs of polystyrene. Leo Fender likely would have approved of the updated wiring, with the second knob now connected to the neck and middle pickups, the third one to the bridge pickup.

Commemorative

Available in 2014 only, the USA-made 60th Anniversary Commemorative Stratocaster combines conventional Strat vibe with modern features and an extra bit of celebratory flash. Historic details include its 2-color burst, vintage-voiced pickups, and vintage-style saddles, while updates include a 2-point trem, Micro-Tilt adjustment, medium jumbo frets, a satin-finish C-shaped neck, and a compound fingerboard that gradually flattens from a chord-friendly 9.5" radius up to a bend-friendly 14". When fully cranked, the no-load feature on the middle and bridge pickups' tone controls removes them altogether from the signal path for maximum Stratitude. Cosmetic touches appropriate to the anniversary celebration include gold hardware, black pearloid dots, pearl-button tuners, a commemorative medallion set into the back of the headstock, and a specially engraved 4-bolt neck plate.

Custom Shop '54 Heavy Relic

For its part, the Custom Shop released the 60th Anniversary 1954 Heavy Relic Stratocaster. Although its scarred and battered wood may exude the vibe of an ancient Viking shield, some features are more modern than their counterparts on the other Anniversary '54, the American Vintage. Specifying the Heavy Relic's details first, then the American Vintage (AV), the two guitars differ in body (1-piece ash vs. 2-piece ash), fingerboard radius (9.5" vs. vintage 7.25"), fret profile (narrow jumbo 6105s vs. vintage), nut width (1.65" vs. 1.625", a 7/10 mm difference), and neck shape (a chunky, broad-shouldered U vs. a C, although both necks are billed as 1954-style). Both guitars have lacquer-finished bodies, 2-color sunbursts, old-school single-ply pickguards, vintage style tuners, and 6-screw vintage tremolos. Both have tone controls for all three pickups, but they go about it in different ways. On the Relic, the third knob is middle/bridge; on the AV, the middle knob is neck/middle.

Connoisseurs will appreciate the Relic's quartersawn neck, finished with a tinted lacquer. Quartersawing first entails the relatively complex and expensive process of sawing a log into quarters, lengthwise; a 10' log is thus split into four 10' quadrants. Unlike vastly more common flat sawn (also "plain" or "slab" sawn) necks, a quartersawn neck is milled so that, as Fender puts it, "the tree's annual growth

rings are perpendicular to the broad face of the boards." Here's another way to think of it: Examine the ends of two necks lying flat on a table. On the flat sawn, the grain lines are horizontal. On the quartersawn, they are vertical, so those grain lines run parallel to the neck's length. Renowned for strength and stability, quartersawn necks are "superior to standard necks in almost every way," according to Fender. (Eric Johnson prefers them, as seen elsewhere in this book.) The Heavy

Relic's other details include a serial number stamped on the tremolo plate in back, a nice touch that hearkens back to the earliest Stratocasters of mid 1954.

In a lengthy and insightful review, *Premier Guitar* magazine Senior Editor Joe Gore examined the Custom Shop Anniversary guitar and wrote: "Does this feel and sound like a fine sexagenarian Strat? Oh my, yes … Everything feels responsive, lively, and nuanced. The neck tone is luscious and warm, but with lots of subtle high-end animation. The bridge setting is unapologetically wiry and bright, but with enough compelling EQ nooks and crannies to keep it from becoming overbearing. The builders did an amazing job distressing the back of the neck to make it feel as if it's endured tens of thousands of hours of spirited playing. I'd defy any blindfolded guitarist to differentiate this artful replica from the real deal." He concluded: "The primal Strat vision in all its glory. Great tones. Great feel. Magnificent neck. This superb guitar feels and sounds as good as any Strat I've played."

The jewel in the 60th Anniversary crown, the pre-beat-to-hell '54 Heavy Relic actually sports several modern features—flatter board, bigger frets, wider nut, and tone controls for all three pickups.

Classic Player '50s

The alder-body 60th Anniversary Classic Player '50s Stratocaster may be the perfect compromise for Strat fans on a budget (not a tiny budget, mind you; it retails for about a grand, still a grand less than the Commemorative version and about $1,500 less than the American Vintage '54). First of all, it looks killer. The charm and appeal of its gold anodized aluminum pickguard on a Desert Sand body go way back to the Musicmaster and Duo-Sonic of the mid-'50s. Gold hardware adds an upscale touch, while aged knobs, stamped saddles, a heel-end rod adjustment, and a gloss nitro-lacquer finish warm up the vintage vibe. Plus, it sounds very good. The pickups are advertised as "American Vintage" Strat units but should not be confused with pickups on any of the Pure Vintage/American Vintage Strats; they are 57/62 American Vintage pickups with a reverse-wound middle unit. Practical features include locking tuners, a 5-way switch, a modern 2-point trem, and a fingerboard with a comfy 9.5" radius and medium jumbo frets.

Years before beginning the 60th Anniversary project, Fender conceived the Classic Player Series as a way to infuse some Custom Shop mojo into more affordable guitars. Justin Norvell: "We had kind of a moat around the Custom Shop, and a lot of their things seemed unattainable for average buyers, so we decided to put a drawbridge across the gap and make some of these advantages more accessible. Three of the Master Builders—Greg Fessler, Dennis Galuszka, and Chris Fleming—went to our Mexico factory with their own ideas. You know, the value in our Master Builders is not just in their hands; it's in their minds—they know what works. So we took some of their expertise and imparted it to the production line."

Greg Fessler: "Most of the changes were minor, but important, nothing crazy. On mine, I flattened out the fingerboard to a 12" radius, swapped out the pickups, and put a 2-point trem on there, to make it a little smoother, a little more modern. We did need the guys in Mexico to clean up some of the body shapes, and they did a great job. I still have the prototype in my office, and it's a great guitar."

The 60th Anniversary Classic Player was derived from Dennis Galuszka's model. Justin Norvell explains that the Classic Players were so successful that some of their features were extended to more expensive series. For example, when the U.S.-made American Series Strat was revised in 2008, Fender replaced the trem with the type that both Galuszka and Fessler had selected for their Mexico-made Classic Players. "We found their bridge of choice to be the best of both worlds," he says, "with vintage-style, bent-steel saddles, but on the modern 2-point fulcrum instead of the 6-screw vintage trem. Every project feeds the next project. Every new thing that we learn gets shared and extended to every appropriate place."

Squier Classic Vibe '50s

The alder-body, gold-on-gold Squier 60th Anniversary Classic Vibe '50s Stratocaster mixes high-glam looks with tough-to-beat value. It offers a gloss-polyester Aztec Gold finish, gold hardware, a 3-ply parchment pickguard, a 6-screw vintage trem, and a stock 5-way switch. The polyester-finished neck sports a C profile, a 9.5" fingerboard radius, and medium jumbo frets. It is the only Anniversary Strat with true vintage wiring: master volume, plus tone controls for the front and middle pickups.

This page: Custom Shop Master Builders contributed to the original Classic Player Series. Opposite: An affordable guitar with quality features and dazzling looks, the Squier Classic Vibe '50s Strat in Aztec Gold.

The TriplePlay HSS

Guitar synthesizers have been around for decades, their performance presumably improving all the time. And yet somehow the enticing possibilities of MIDI, synthesis, and sampling—long harnessed to good effect by keyboardists—have seemed just out of reach. Skilled trade-show

often rendered these wonderful-in-theory devices less than wonderful in reality.

If anyone could make them work, it might well be Larry Fishman. A veteran of more than three decades in the music business, he cofounded Parker guitars, co-designed the revolutionary Parker Fly guitar, and partnered with Guild, Martin and other industry leaders. His company has designed and marketed highly regarded pickups, preamps, acoustic

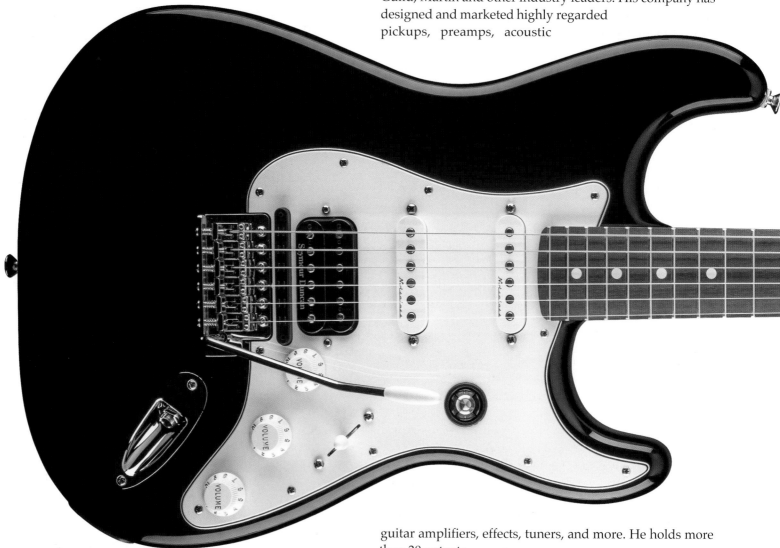

demonstrators and a few committed artists have used commercially available controllers to explore new sonic realms, but for some of us, guitar synthesizers never seemed to work so well. Glitches, tracking bugs, delayed responses, and other ghosts and goblins in the machine

guitar amplifiers, effects, tuners, and more. He holds more than 30 patents.

A collaboration with Fender resulted in the Fender Fishman TriplePlay Stratocaster HSS. Fender calls it "the Stratocaster of the future, a phenomenal leap forward," and the guitar does seem to be incandescent with potential. First, a bit of background. Larry Fishman: "I previously worked with practically every synth manufacturer on the planet. I have almost every guitar synth ever made in my lab, from all around the world, and 99 percent of the companies who made those things are out of business. So early on, I understood the challenges and shortcomings of MIDI. At the same time, I always saw the promise. The problem was, it took a magician to play one without glitches; performance was hit or miss. If all you ever did was to play notes, some of the older devices could work okay, but of course playing guitar is all about bending, sliding, hammering on, pulling off, and so on, so the computer has to make very quick decisions about reproducing what you're playing, and this requires major computational power."

At first Larry Fishman remained doubtful about MIDI guitar because so many previous users had been burned by their experiences, but several crucial advances changed his mind. A guitar synth system requires some sort of divided/hex pickup, and Larry Fishman's piezo-based

the unlimited potential of software." This application of wireless technology enabled jettisoning not only hardware-based sound modules but also previously required accessories such as heavy, 13-pin cables with special connectors. With the TriplePlay, all the processing and MIDI conversion is done with the onboard processor, powered by a rechargeable lithium ion battery. This streaming MIDI data is sent to a computer, tablet or other device and triggers the software-based sounds.

Now you can tap into the unique character of the Fender Stratocaster while also accessing tens of thousands of virtual instruments—Hammond organs, orchestral violins, vocal choirs, basses, reeds, brass, percussion—and that's only the beginning. You can also conjure nonmusical sound effects, make multitrack recordings, create loops, and even assign the software to reproduce what you're playing in standard notation on a musical staff for archiving, copyright, or rehearsal applications.

products had been improving that technology for years. For Fender, he devised a thin magnetic unit that houses six tiny humbuckers, one for each string, and sits between the bridge/tailpiece and bridge pickup. The Strat was ideal because its design allows the hex pickup to be positioned close to the bridge, which makes for optimal tracking.

Another step was developing a strong proficiency with a powerful microprocessor called a Blackfin, made by Analog Devices. "Also," Larry reports, "a guy who works for me, Andras Szalay, is probably the world's leading expert on pitch detection. We realized we could transmit a robust signal of MIDI data to a little receiver *wirelessly,* very quickly, and that way the processor is right on the guitar. That was the key. I did not want to be tied to having a hardware box with a few hundred sounds that you would get bored with after a while, so we spent another year developing a software interface, and then you could access

The guitar's wireless MIDI data is accompanied by signals from a trio of magnetic pickups familiar to many a guitarist—a Seymour Duncan Pearly Gates humbucker and a pair of Fender's Vintage Noiseless single-coils. You can send those signals from the standard output jack through a standard cable to a standard amp. You can also send the pickups' signals through the supplied USB cable to your computer. And, you can do both at the same time, using the volume controls on the guitar to blend synthesized flutes or clavinets or what have you with the pure Strat tones. The three knobs look stock, but on this guitar they control master volume, MIDI volume, and headphone-monitor volume. (An extra output jack accommodates the headphones.)

The included USB flash drive provides all the necessary software for recording, editing, and playing back your music. Larry Fishman: "This is a wonderful opportunity, a gateway for guitarists to get involved in the digital world with implications for learning, practicing, teaching, recording, and performing. I hope that among other things it will renew interest in guitar for a generation of musicians already fluent with computers." Justin Norvell adds: "Developments in equipment and developments in gear affect each other in a circular way. When distortion and high volume came out, feedback was added to the musical mix. The Floyd Rose created new possibilities. We think the TriplePlay will encourage players to explore new sonic realms."

Deluxe HSS Plus Top With iOS Connectivity

Looking at the more or less century-long evolution of the electric guitar, we've properly acknowledged dozens of innovations, some of them radical. And yet the technological leaps of just the last decade or two are so astounding they make the previous hundred years look almost like a refinement of a single idea: Take an electrical connecting cord and stick one end into a guitar with transducers of some sort and the other end into an amplifier. With iOS, the interface Operating System that powers Apple's mobile devices, you can use your cell phone or digital pad to replace amps, stompboxes, metronomes, tuners, samplers, storage devices, instructional videos, and tape or digital recorders. You can use your touch screen to replace at least some aspects of brick-and-mortar retail stores. Accessing hundreds of thousands of amplifier tones, effects, and speaker emulators; rerouting your signal chain with infinite flexibility; using a single handheld device for learning, transposing, songwriting, rehearsing, recording, mixing, monitoring, emulating other instruments, or performing with backing tracks in any style or with other musicians in real time, perhaps on different continents—we weren't even dreaming of such things until recently.

It's all exhilarating, and potentially overwhelming. David Torn once invoked a computer-user term, "option anxiety," in reference to the plethora of sonic possibilities encountered by guitarists. And that was two or three decades ago. Manufacturers today are faced not only with developing new gear but also with responding to players'

real-world priorities, and with balancing some products' mindboggling versatility with their ease of use. And there remains a deeply rooted perception, at least among players of a certain age, that Leo Fender, Les Paul, Ted McCarty, and their contemporaries already thought up the best ideas in guitars, basses and amps in the middle of the last century. For them, a tap, a swipe, and a pinch may never replace twiddling a knob or stepping on a footswitch. Besides, everybody knows transistors don't sound as good as tubes, digital isn't as warm as analog, etc. And yet *Premier Guitar* magazine Senior Editor Joe Gore, himself a deeply experienced musician, wrote in 2014 that the best iOS music apps not only offer practical interfaces and smooth connectivity but also "shockingly good sound."

Fender figured that more than a few players would crave access to the digital multiverse but wouldn't want to give up the vibe and the tactile experience that drew them to the guitar in the first place. An ideal solution might be the moderately priced Deluxe Stratocaster HSS Plus Top With iOS Connectivity. That mouthful of a model name describes a Strat that looks conventional but performs like no other. Plug it into your amp like any electric guitar and wallow in the joys of playing a fancy, flame-top Strat with a C-shaped neck, a 9.5"-radius fingerboard, a 2-point trem, and an HSS pickup array—hum/single/single. Or, access a zillion musician-oriented apps by using the onboard USB interface to connect directly to an iOS device such as your iPad, iPod, iPhone, or computer. A handy headphone output jack is also built in; the guitar's third knob looks stock but functions as a headphone volume control. Whether your preference runs to amps or apps, the iOS Strat covers all bases. Gorgeous, too.

...looks conventional but performs like no other.

Buckeye Burl

Wow. This striking Fender is topped with bookmatched buckeye burl and features a "flamed ash" back, a pair of TV Jones Gretsch-style Power'Tron pickups, and a spectacular AAAA flame maple neck. Master Builder Dale Wilson: "I built it as a one-off showpiece for the 2014 NAMM Show and have received some orders since then. I make them one at a time. I thought the green abalone dots would go with the buckeye burl, which is a California fruit wood. The Power'Trons make this Stratocaster sound very meaty, with a nice thick tone. They make anything sound good."

This gold-leaf Strat is called the Sakura, after the cherry blossom motif created by Troy Lee Designs. It is pictured here on the spot where it came to life, the workbench of Master Builder Dale Wilson. The peghead features gold leaf on black lacquer. The flowers on the fingerboard may look random at first, but they are functional position markers. "The way the flowers spill over from the ebony board onto the gold-leaf body is just beautiful," says Dale. "Troy Lee Designs is right here in Corona and does all sorts of sportswear, motorcycle gas tanks, racing helmets—exciting stuff with custom paint and custom lettering. This was a joint project. Gold leaf is always difficult to apply, but with the flower motif it was even more challenging; very few people could pull this off." Gold hardware complements the artwork.

Master Builder Dale Wilson with one of his creations, a maple-top, green-burst Strat with a pickguard of single-ply pearloid. The neck was shaped from a block of solid rosewood, with a rosewood fingerboard. "I love oiled necks," says Wilson. "It's unusual for Fender, but the whole idea was to do something different. The Seymour Duncan lipstick pickups ended up sounding really good in this guitar."

Built by Dale Wilson for the 2013 NAMM Show, this stunner features a AAAA quilted maple top, a natural-finished AAAA quilted maple pickguard, a Sienna burst finish, gold hardware, a rosewood board, and a neck crafted from a knockout piece of bird's-eye maple.

Give Me Liberty

Built for a 2013 NAMM Show, the Liberty Strat (also called the Colonial) quotes a line from fiery orator Patrick Henry's most famous speech and evokes Benjamin Franklin's famous "Join or Die" woodcut political cartoon, which represented the American colonies' disunited state at the time. The guitar was a collaboration between Master Builder Dale Wilson and artist Frank Germano, of Man On Fire Design. Wilson chose a hardtail bridge so the hand-painted artwork on the back wouldn't be obstructed by a trem cover. "Frank came in with a rough drawing," he recalls, "and it looked great. I wanted the guitar to have an old colonial look, in keeping with the theme, but not too trashed, so this is more of a light relic. I protected the artwork with nitro lacquer over the body." Note the highly figured bird's-eye maple neck and fingerboard.

Because it was an election year and the guitar was being unveiled close to inauguration time, Frank Germano wanted something that spoke to national pride. "However," he says, "I didn't want it to feel like it leaned either right or left. I wanted something everyone could get behind. I didn't use red, white, and blue, or stars and stripes, or any of that more typical imagery. Instead, I took a lead from a time when the U.S. was forming, a time well before our modern party lines."

He started by doing the aging effects around the pickguard edges, bridge, output jack, etc. A bit of freehand pencil drawing helped get the shapes in the right place and provided a guide for the artwork. He laid down all the black, and finished up with metallic gold highlights. The paint is acrylic except for the brightest metallic gold parts, which were done in enamel. "It's really the only way to get the best brightness and opacity," he explains. "There are acrylic highlights as well, but they're more transparent. I hand-painted the yellowing effects on the undercoat, and Dale brought it home with the relicing."

Germano aimed for an overall style with a hand-finished, folk-art feel, as if the guitar had been around for a while and had some history of its own. "More than anything else," he says, "I wanted it to look like someone might have found it in the corner of an old barn in Tennessee, a special piece of Americana that was lovingly created a very long time ago, lived an amazing life of musical adventure, was for some reason forgotten, and then randomly found and appreciated in a whole new way."

Right: A sketch for the back's artwork.

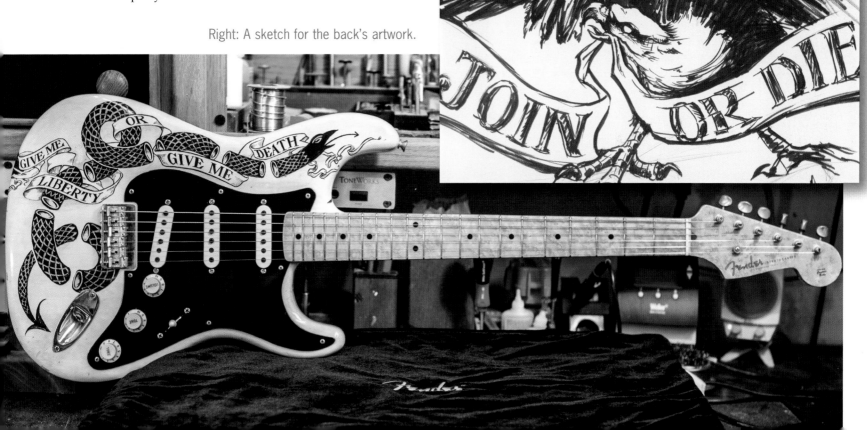

Midnight Opulence
A Collaboration of
Old World Masters

Custom Shop Master Builder Yuriy Shishkov wanted to make a guitar bedecked with diamonds and other precious stones, and with silver and gold wire. "I didn't have any particular concept in mind at the beginning," he says. "I simply wanted to think of the guitar's top almost like a canvas, and do something more abstract than a classic scroll or floral motif. The deep purplish blue reflects the 'midnight' theme." Yuriy drew the right half of the symmetrical design directly onto the top. He then traced it, flipped it over, and drew the mirror image on the left-hand side.

"Working with the silver and gold wire is slow and painstaking," he explains. "I used a tool with a blade like a microscopic chisel or a scalpel, but instead of cutting a channel and removing wood, you're just pressing the blade into the wood and piercing it, making a slit about 1/16 of an inch deep. Each time you move forward, you are only going an increment of about 1/64 of an inch. The wire is not round. It's a flat ribbon, approximately nine thousandths thick. You hammer it in on its side, so all you see is the thickness of the wire, which is much thinner than the one-millimeter width. The art is to make the lines flowing in continuous curves, without elbows or angles or breaks."

Yuriy was asked if some of the work on 2012's Midnight Opulence Stratocaster—particularly the design near the center of the fingerboard—reflected his Russian heritage. "If any of the work I do resembles art from Russia, it's probably more of a genetic thing than anything intended to represent Russian folk art. That's just the background I inherited from my culture back in the USSR."

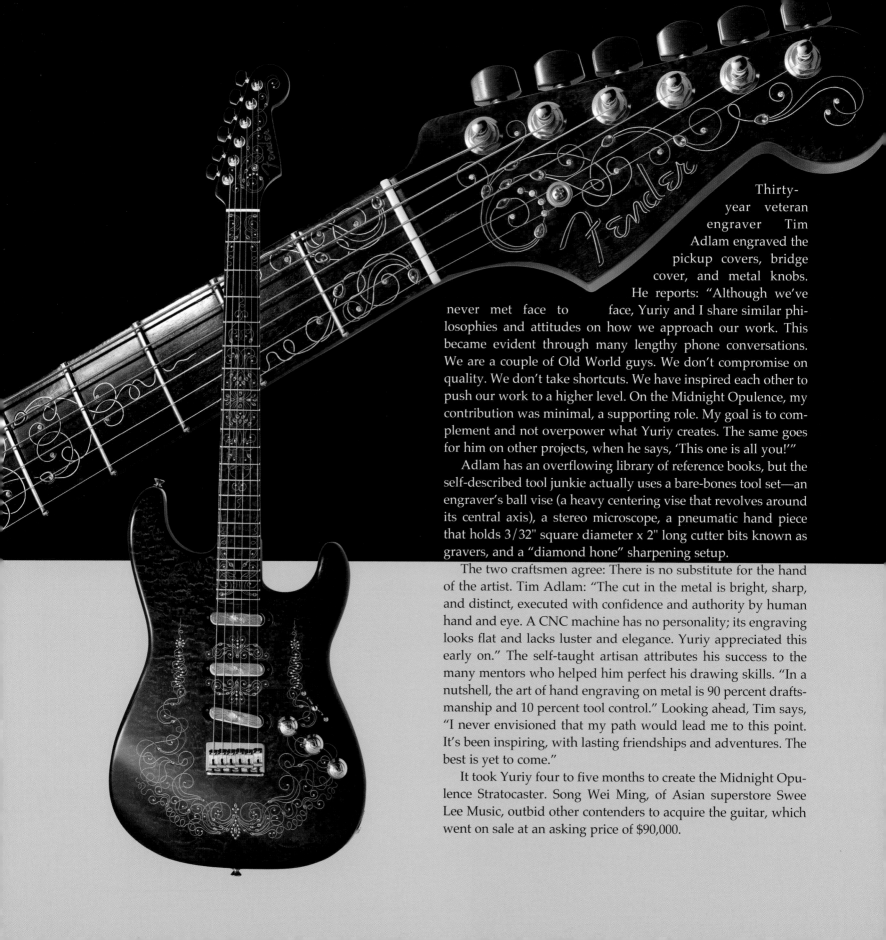

Thirty-year veteran engraver Tim Adlam engraved the pickup covers, bridge cover, and metal knobs. He reports: "Although we've never met face to face, Yuriy and I share similar philosophies and attitudes on how we approach our work. This became evident through many lengthy phone conversations. We are a couple of Old World guys. We don't compromise on quality. We don't take shortcuts. We have inspired each other to push our work to a higher level. On the Midnight Opulence, my contribution was minimal, a supporting role. My goal is to complement and not overpower what Yuriy creates. The same goes for him on other projects, when he says, 'This one is all you!'"

Adlam has an overflowing library of reference books, but the self-described tool junkie actually uses a bare-bones tool set—an engraver's ball vise (a heavy centering vise that revolves around its central axis), a stereo microscope, a pneumatic hand piece that holds 3/32" square diameter x 2" long cutter bits known as gravers, and a "diamond hone" sharpening setup.

The two craftsmen agree: There is no substitute for the hand of the artist. Tim Adlam: "The cut in the metal is bright, sharp, and distinct, executed with confidence and authority by human hand and eye. A CNC machine has no personality; its engraving looks flat and lacks luster and elegance. Yuriy appreciated this early on." The self-taught artisan attributes his success to the many mentors who helped him perfect his drawing skills. "In a nutshell, the art of hand engraving on metal is 90 percent draftsmanship and 10 percent tool control." Looking ahead, Tim says, "I never envisioned that my path would lead me to this point. It's been inspiring, with lasting friendships and adventures. The best is yet to come."

It took Yuriy four to five months to create the Midnight Opulence Stratocaster. Song Wei Ming, of Asian superstore Swee Lee Music, outbid other contenders to acquire the guitar, which went on sale at an asking price of $90,000.

Yuriy Shishkov named the one-off Hermitage Stratocaster in honor of one of the world's greatest art collections, at the State Hermitage in St. Petersburg, Russia. Its dazzling gems look like they could have adorned the Imperial Crown at the Winter Palace: 556 diamonds, 281 emeralds, 100 rubies, and 70 sapphires—1,007 precious stones in all. Yuriy Shishkov: "This guitar represents not only true treasures of diamonds, rubies, sapphires, and emeralds, but also the architectural design elements of the world-famous palace."

Although the Hermitage Stratocaster of 2014 helped commemorate the Strat's 60th birthday, it was not one of the official Anniversary models and did not bear an Anniversary label. As we go to press, Yuriy acknowledged reports that Fender received an offer of one million dollars for the jewel-encrusted artwork/instrument. "The status is still open," he explained in 2014. "An offer was made, but it was not Fender's intention to sell the guitar right away. I heard there is more than one person who wants to obtain it."

Facing page: The Featherlight's pickups were a collaboration with Yuriy Shishkov, the legendary pickup guru Abigail Ybarra, and her apprentice, Josefina Campos, a veteran with more than 20 years' experience at the company. In May 2013, the much-loved Abigail retired after more than a half-century at Fender. After a three-year apprenticeship with Abby, Josefina succeeded her mentor.

Master Builder Yuriy Shishkov's aptly named Featherlight Stratocaster of 2014 was an experiment that turned out even better than its creator had hoped. Perhaps the 4-pound guitar's most distinctive feature is the neck, crafted not from any of the traditional neck woods but rather from quarter-sawn, aircraft-grade spruce. Yuriy Shishkov: "It is much, much lighter than maple, and at the same time structurally stronger. That's why it's been used on airplanes and also on braces for acoustic guitars. Spruce is stiff, but it's also soft and wouldn't hold frets, so I went with a round-lam rosewood fingerboard."

The body was crafted from polonia, also called empress wood. "It's very light," Yuriy says, "and it sounds really good. You might say it's more of a woody tone; acoustically it's very projective. Polonia is strong but soft, so these are hardtails. If I installed a tremolo, the weight would defeat the purpose. I would also have to reinforce the attachment area, another increase in weight. It's a unique guitar, so I wanted special pickups for it. Everybody who played a Featherlight loved the sound. I made quite a few because it's been quite popular."

Milestone: The Eric Johnson Strat

An interview with Eric Johnson and Michael Frank-Braun

Eric Johnson's ears are so good, he can tell the difference between Coke and Pepsi by the sound of the fizz. That's just one of the jokes about a man who hears things the rest of us just don't hear. He is discriminating and precise, to be sure (he removes the rear cover plate from his Strats, not only because he wants to avoid pesky alignment issues when changing strings but also because he thinks it improves the sound, which, when you think about it, makes sense), and yet he will tell you that his obsessive-nitpicker persona has been blown way out of proportion. As it turns out, the real Eric Johnson pretty much wants the same things we all do—a reliable guitar that sounds great, stays in tune, is comfortable to play, works well with rhythms and leads, and drives pedals in a good way while also providing the rich glassy tones that make a Stratocaster one of the world's most distinctive guitar voices. Working on a signature model with an artist who is almost as legendary for his ears as for his hands was an inspiring learning experience for all concerned.

Michael Frank-Braun was born in Germany and grew up on the music of the artists he heard on American radio—Cream, the Beatles, Miles Davis, and many more. His dad repaired tube radios, so young Michael was around music-related technology during his formative years. He modified the guitars his parents bought for him, worked for other musicians as well, started his own guitar line in Hamburg (the Scorpions' Matthias Jabs was one customer), moved to Canada in 1990, and joined Fender R&D in 1997. He has led several development projects for Fender and worked with Jimmie Vaughan, Marcus Miller, Victor Bailey, Bonnie Raitt, and many more. As we go to press, his current title is Principal Engineer. Michael Frank-Braun: "Collaborating with Eric Johnson was a great experience, and we both learned a lot. I have all the respect for Eric. Some of the things he believes in go into the mystic philosophy area, but at the same time, on many of these technical things he was dead right."

You have spent years comparing the design, materials, and construction of Stratocasters. Have you written down all this information, made notes about your preferences, or do you carry it in your head?

Eric: I thought about writing a book on tone, just a little handbook, something I could pass down to anyone who is interested, but my thinking has progressed over the years. I used to be under the assumption that everything has to be perfect, and I finally realized, you know what? You can't really calculate or formulate a lot of it.

Fender had been talking about doing an Eric Johnson model for a long time. How did the initial contact finally come about?

Eric: I had declined a few times, but when I met Michael Frank-Braun, we had a long talk. He's from a European, Old World craftsmanship point of view, and he understood where I was coming from and was the perfect guy to put this thing together.

Michael Frank-Braun is highly regarded as a pickup designer; was he also involved in other aspects of the model?

Eric: Oh, yes, all sorts of things. He brought a lot of things into reality and is very much responsible for helping to make this guitar a good one. We did it together. We started out by spec-ing out this really good '57 I have, and everything went from there. We experimented with the distance between the strings and ended up with a vintage trem. We looked at how much of a V we wanted on the back of the neck, and we shaped the body to be a little bit more like some of the earlier '50s guitars. I knew I wanted a flatter radius, more like a Gibson, and bigger frets. I wanted a little hotter bridge pickup; that's always an issue with me.

Michael Frank-Braun: The tremolo block was probably the place where we made the most discoveries, and it improved the guitar's overall sound. Remember that the drilled holes have two diameters. The big one lets the ball end go through, and then the string goes up through the smaller hole to the saddle. Remember the Bullet strings? They had the longer brass ending instead of the usual ball. They were supposed to improve the stability of the tremolo. In the block, Fender lengthened the countersink to accommodate the Bullets. The thinking was that the regular ball might move around a little, but the bullet would lock in flush and tight in its channel. Over time the holes had gotten deeper, and the deeper they get, the more steel gets taken from that bridge block, and that makes a difference in the sound. Eric pointed out that on some guitars, like on Jimi Hendrix's Strat, you could see the ends of the strings in back, the ball ends, so the holes were shallow. So we went to a shorter depth, with more mass remaining in the block. That improves the sound.

Changing the paint on the tremolo block—can someone really tell a difference in sound?

Michael: Actually, that was a significant change. At some point the silver paint was replaced by silver powder coat on the American Standard, and it sometimes was used on some vintage bridges. The top surface of the block was not supposed to be coated, but when we changed vendors, the

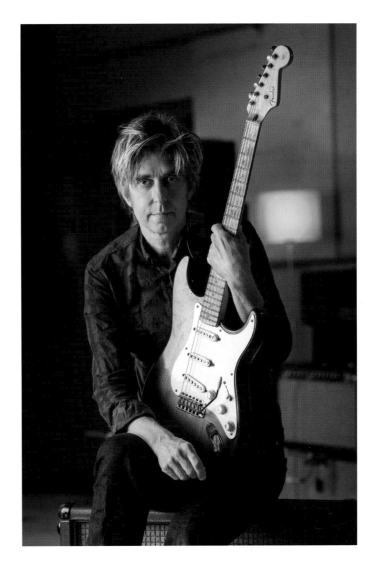

"Pickup design is like a negotiation."
— Eric Johnson

whole block got coated by mistake. I sanded the powder coat off and mounted the base plate metal to metal. That improved the sound and added more sparkle to the tone. Eric wanted to return to the silver paint except with no paint at all where the block joins the base plate.

The Strat you played for many years, nicknamed Virginia, was a '54. But it sounds like vintage authenticity was not a high priority for your signature model.

Eric: I've given up on that. Virginia wasn't stock, either, not at all. I flattened the board and put big frets on it, changed the tuning keys, rewired the electronics. I sold that guitar years ago. I don't know what I was thinking, what my problem was. Stupid move. After that I tried to get all these vintage guitars, but that was me trying to fit into some clothes that didn't fit. Those guitars were totally stock, and I respected that and honored that, but they just weren't as much fun to play. I've made peace with the fact that I don't really want a 100 percent vintage Strat anymore.

What was the problem with the stock originals?

Eric: The bridge pickup was always too weak for me, so I would struggle with that, but one day I finally said, you know what? I guess I'm not a pure vintage guy, so I took that pickup out and put in a hotter one. I thought, at the end of the day, I should be doing music and maybe not obsessing quite so much about vintage.

Was that the DiMarzio?

Eric: Yeah, I liked that HS-2, but I didn't hook up that bottom coil; I just left it single-coil. It's from the '80s. I also used a pickup that Fender made for me, basically just a Fender alnico [aluminum, nickel, cobalt] 5 that's wrapped to about 6.8 or 6.9 [DC resistance, in k-ohms] instead of 5.8. That rating is only one of the many things that go into the sound of a pickup and how it plays clean and how it distorts. There's a whole bunch of factors—magnets, wire, voltage, current. But with the little bit I knew, that higher rating works better, at least for me. It was a better lead tone. The Fenders at 5.8, I could never get them to have enough gain on a lead tone, whether it was the 5.8 rating or something else.

Michael: On the Eric Johnson guitar, each pickup is tailored for its location under the strings, and all three are different. Eric had a '54 Strat with alnico 3 magnets. The alnico 3 has the lowest magnetic pull because there is no cobalt—they should have called it just alni instead of

alnico [laughs]. It makes a beautiful neck pickup because it doesn't pull the string quite so much and has a larger magnetic field. The sound is mellow but not muddy. And we looked at the OD—Outside Diameter—and tried different measurements. If you go up in size another 10/1000ths or so, it's going to have a different magnetic field and a little different sound.

And the middle pickup?

Michael: Alnico 2, and no tone control. Eric has a unique approach. He wants that middle pickup to be low because of his fingerpicking. That meant we needed more gain because it was further from the strings. We made it reverse-polarity so that it's hum-canceling. The basic approach was getting a pickup with enough gain and crunch and percussion, and that's also why the middle pickup has no tone control. That was very deliberate. That gives positions 2 and 4 a really nice sparkling sound because it doesn't have the second 250k load of a tone control. A 250k volume control plus a 250k tone control gives you a 125k load, because the controls are parallel. The tonality of the pickup can really change with a different load.

And the bridge?

Michael: This was the most problematic because Eric wanted a lot of gain to drive the Fuzz Face in front of his Marshall, but also when the guitar is in position 2 it's supposed to be sparkling. We went with alnico 5 for the bridge pickup with some additional turns of wire.

There are rumors about how many sets of pickups went back and forth before you finally settled on ones you liked.

Eric: There were a lot. It's always a trade-off. Every time you gain something, you lose a little something somewhere else, so pickup design is like a negotiation. You are trying to get a better lead tone without losing something on that crystal clear rhythm tone, so I was trying to find a balance where you could have a twangy clean tone and more of a woody lead tone.

Michael: I have about three-and-a-half boxes of Eric Johnson prototype pickups, with 50 or so in each box, so it was like 180 pickups [laughs]. To a large degree they were all tested by Eric. The only exceptions were when we thought we were moving in the wrong direction, so I might hold back a few samples I had already made. I sent him complete pickguard assemblies which he could drop into the guitar with a fast change. Eric is very systematic, and we did so much research.

Aside from the different magnets, what makes these pickups distinctive?

Michael: We discovered that when Leo ordered Fender's typical 42-gauge Formvar wire [with polyvinyl formal insulating film], the measuring wasn't so precise back then. It could vary around the 42 gauge standard. Elektrisola is a very good German-based company with a facility in New Hampshire. I worked closely with a lead engineer there. Elektrisola works in millimeters, and within that range of 42-gauge Formvar wire, they have six different gauges, so we could tailor the sound extremely precisely to the sound and response Eric was looking for; because of the laser technology today, we are able to repeat it precisely in production. And then of course the thickness of the coating is very important. We tried three different ones: G1, G2, and G3. The size of the magnets is another consideration. All these physical things have an impact on the sound. We stuck with the .063 wire gauge for each pickup, which we now call the Eric Johnson wire, and we went with the thinnest coating.

For your own model, what were you looking for, specifically?

Eric: One thing, we went round and round to get the right kind of pickup that would trigger an overdrive pedal in a musical way. Some pickups have a tendency to be stiff and unrelenting, and others really just work better with a fuzz or an overdrive. I wanted to get rid of the string tree, because I always felt that was a source of tuning problems. I also wanted to add a tone control to the bridge pickup.

It's ironic that one of the greatest vintage guitars of all time has no tone control for the lead pickup.

Eric: Right, and people have been solving that in different ways for a lot of years. On my guitar, we have the master

Michael Frank-Braun: "Eric is very systematic, and we did so much research."

volume, plus tone controls for the bridge pickup and neck pickup.

You prefer maple-neck boards?

Eric: Yes, and the necks are quartersawn. I haven't done a super amount of experimenting with quartersawn necks and other necks, but I noticed over the years a higher percentage of guitars I liked seemed to be quartersawn. [Note: Please see the discussion of quartersawn necks in the section addressing the Custom Shop's 60th Anniversary Heavy Relic '54, pp. 44-45.]

Michael: Leo almost always used flat-sawn, which has the advantage of making the truss rod easier to adjust, but for some strange reason, the neck on Eric's 57 was partially quartersawn. You don't see true, 90-degree quartersawn very often; there's usually a bit of an angle in quartersawn. It's not a good thing or a bad thing; it's just different. It gives, in my opinion, a little bit more of a crunch sound.

The note has more of a percussive impact with the first hit of the pick. With the flat-sawn, I think the neck may be moving a little bit more, and that may be why it has a little bit of a softer attack. But remember, we are talking about wood, so each neck has a little different approach anyway. We made several prototypes, about seven or eight, and the one with the quartersawn neck did seem to have that ability to cut through a band. But it's all a matter of taste.

The common wisdom is that maple boards have a brighter sound.

Eric: I think they do, but it's more about the tonality being a little purer. When you play a note you get more of a focus. With rosewood, the harmonics are more jumbled up, which in some ways you can really use to your advantage, but in the bigger picture for me, I like to have it pure in the fundamental.

Michael: The bone nut makes a difference, of course, and the Eric Johnson model was the first time we used it on a factory production guitar. They use them all the time over in the Custom Shop. The bone nut just has a more defined tone but it's also a warm sound. It's a beautiful thing to have. All these things work together.

The rosewood-board versions have neck binding, like the Strats pictured in the 1966-'67 catalog, very unusual for Fender.

Eric: A lot of people don't know about those guitars. They are so rare. I always thought the binding just looked so cool. Ry Cooder has one. I don't know if anybody knows how many were made. I don't think I've ever seen one in person. On the Eric Johnson guitars the rosewood necks are the round-lam type.

What are some things on your personal guitars that didn't make it onto the EJ models?

Eric: On my own guitars, I lean the strings a bit toward the bass side so there's a little more room on the fingerboard on the 1st-string side than on the 6th-string side. When I'm doing bends and pulloffs, I don't worry about pushing the string over the edge. I will move the nut over or have a new nut made. But the basics are all there, and the [Eric Johnson model] is really different than anything else they offer.

Are you able to take these signature Fenders to the gig and have them work for you?

Eric: Yeah, I am. I've got a nice maple-neck one I really like. I can go to the store and get one, and it's ready to play. Every guitar is different. They all vary, but there's a level of consistency that's impressive, and it's got all the appointments I like. The pickups have improved in recent years, so the newest ones are better than ever. Fender is on a roll.

Vice President Justin Norvell, on creating the Eric Johnson Stratocaster: "Eric Johnson's ear is fine-tuned, to say the least. We made so many different sets of pickups for him to try. Some were radically different from each other, but others had the most discrete, minute differences you can imagine, the tiniest tweaks. People talk about the big things, like a pickup's output, and we considered those things, too, but a PAF and a single-coil Tele pickup can have the same output, but that doesn't mean they are going to sound alike. We went way, way beyond all that and looked at things like shellacking vs. wax-potting the pickups, and even the temperature at which we wax-potted the pickups, to see if those things would have any effect on the pickup's performance. That deep journey we took with Eric was a reinvigoration of our approach to every conceivable detail on these guitars."

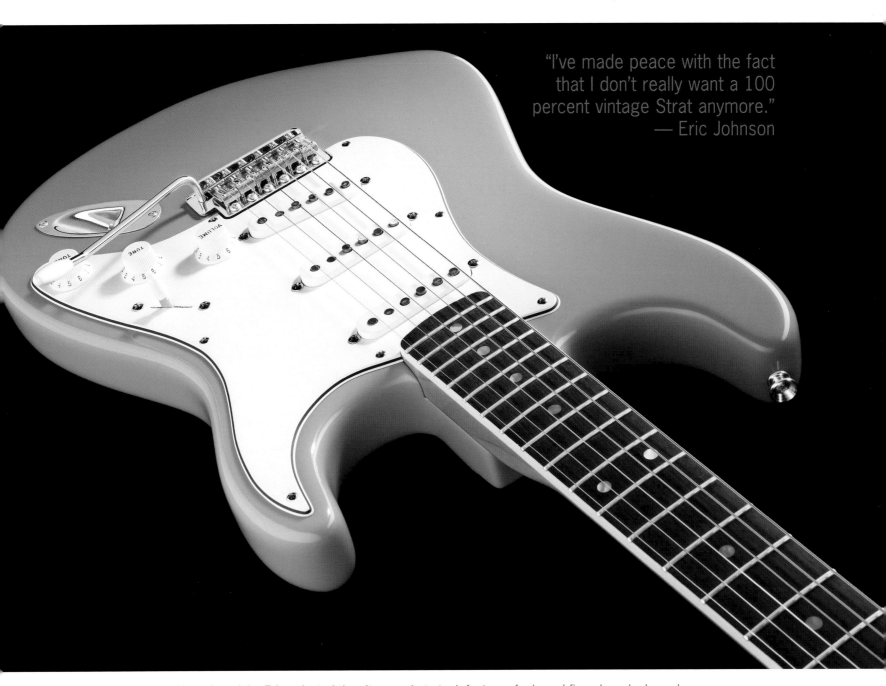

"I've made peace with the fact that I don't really want a 100 percent vintage Strat anymore."
— Eric Johnson

For the rosewood-board models, Eric selected the ultra-rare but stock feature of a bound fingerboard, shown here on a gorgeous EJ Strat in Tropical Turquoise.

The KWS Orange Sparkle Strat

Kenny Wayne Shepherd's reverse-headstock Strat was built by Todd Krause. "My favorite color is orange," Todd says, "so when Kenny told me he wanted an orange guitar, I said, you're talking to the right guy. Later I was thinking, man, sparkle would be cool, but I was reluctant to suggest it because sparkle is something you either like or don't. People aren't neutral about it. Kenny and I went back and forth on all these details, and then I get this e-mail out of the blue—is it too late to do a sparkle [laughs]? I thought, great coincidence, so I did this orange sparkle that just lights up. If the sunlight hits it, or stage lights, it looks like it's crawling; that's the only way I can explain it. Did you ever see a million red ants swarming out of an anthill? This orange sparkle finish *moves*."

While most details are right side up, the trem bar location, bridge-pickup slant, and headstock are upside down. Any Strat with a reverse headstock is bound to suggest some sort of Jimi Hendrix connection, and this guitar was conceived precisely for the purpose of playing Hendrix songs in concert. However striking, the reverse headstock entails a lot more than appearance. The longer treble strings and shorter bass strings affect both sound and feel.

"It makes a difference, absolutely," says Todd Krause. "A lot of people underestimate string length's effect on tone. The longer the string, the heavier gauge you can use, the thicker the sounds. If you take a guitar scale and extend it to 36", see what happens? Now it's a bass, with huge strings. Your E will be all the way down in a different octave.

"By the way, if you want to play Hendrix, you need to tune down, like Jimi did. It changes the string tension. Otherwise it won't sound right. String tension, gauge, length—all these things work together. Stevie Ray tuned down, too. Kenny's strings are relatively big to start with, normally with a .012 and then a really heavy low E. I don't do that sort of thing on my own guitars because I figure, I'm never going to sound like Jimi no matter what I do [laughs], so give me a set of 10s and let's keep it simple."

Look past the eye-poppin' glitz, and you'll see several functional details that make this an ideal guitar for conjuring the sound and style of Jimi Hendrix.

Blender Fender
A '63 With a Twist

The Master Design 1963 Relic Stratocaster was conceived and built by Master Builder John Cruz. He explains: "The assignment was, build your guitar, exactly the way you want it, but if other people want the same thing, we can offer it as a Team Built, so it's a neat combination approach. My birth year is 1963, and it's also a very special year for Strats." This guitar reflected a strategy Cruz had

pursued before: stock looks, but with surprises lurking under the hood. On his personal Strats he rarely uses the third knob, leaving it fully cranked most or all of the time. To squeeze additional versatility out of his Master Design, he converted that knob into a blend control. You can combine the neck and bridge pickups for a near-Tele type tone; or, depending on the settings on the stock 5-way,

"It plays like an old friend."

you can blend all three pickups, which gives a sound much to John's liking as well. "I tried the blend on my guitar at home and really liked it," he says. "It was great for rhythm sounds, clean sounds. It's also great for soloing with the neck and bridge pickups together. You can fade in exactly however much you want of the other pickup."

The trem bar is a little thicker than normal, heavier-duty. "I have a tendency to get a little nuts with my bar every once in a while," John laughs. "I've broken off many arms, and it's a pain to get the broken piece out of the block. I ruined a few. I've read about how they did some custom bars for Stevie Ray and thought it would be a good idea for the Master Design, so I have them specially machined. It feels a lot better in my hand, but it still looks stock, other than the diameter being a little bigger."

The trem block is different as well. A pal who does Floyd Rose upgrades sent John a number of parts fabricated from brass, titanium, and other metals. After some experimentation, John settled on brass for the trem block. "I found it livened up the sound," he says, "so I incorporated that to get a bit of extra texture to the sound." Cosmetics include a 3-ply mint green pickguard on a 2-color sunburst (actually a mid-'50s color).

The neck is quartersawn maple. John Cruz adds: "I also like round-lam boards with big frets, and the radius is 12", pretty flat, because I have a tendency to bend a lot. The C-shape neck is a little bit larger, as I've got bigger hands. The roll on the edge of the fretboard has a very nice, broken-in feel, very comfortable. It plays like an old friend."

Gobsmacked

Recreating The Shadows / Hank Marvin Strat

Although The Shadows were formed as the backup band for late-'50s/early-'60s teen idol Cliff Richard, sometimes loosely described as the British Elvis, they went on to lasting fame on their own as an instrumental supergroup. Lead guitarist Hank Marvin would become the UK's first true guitar hero.

Cliff Richard purchased a Stratocaster for Hank to play. Believed to be the first Strat imported into Great Britain, the red Fender with gold-plated hardware absolutely floored England's guitar community upon its arrival and became indelibly associated with the iconic guitarist. Bruce Welch, Hank's co-guitarist in "The Shads," later acquired it from Cliff.

The Custom Shop's Limited Edition Dealer Select 1959 Custom Red CRS-59 Stratocaster of 2009 is perhaps better known as the 50th Anniversary Shadows guitar, a tribute to both Hank Marvin and his legendary Fender. The project was conceived and commissioned by Howard Gillespie of Oasis Music in Ringwood, Hampshire, England. Fender had previously released signature Strats associated with the bespectacled

At some point in the mid-'60s, Cliff Richard had the guitar refinished in white (let us now pause to groan in unison), and in the 1970s Bruce Welch had it refinished yet again in red, obliterating all traces of the factory paint. So, the only guidelines to duplicating the original color were the opinions of people who remembered it a half-century later. Input came from Bruce Welch, Hank Marvin, and Terrence "Jet" Harris, The Shadows' founding bassist.

For years before historians unearthed and published Fender's official color charts, collectors and players invoked several unofficial nicknames that Fender never used (salmon pink, for example). Howard Gillespie told *Guitar Buyer* magazine: "Both Bruce and Hank are adamant that the guitar was a flamingo pink color and not Fiesta Red, and we went to great lengths to get the color right."

At this point we will engage in a bit of informed speculation. The original color may have been Fiesta Red as far as Fender was concerned (which wasn't all that far by purist standards),   and it may also have been unique: The two   are not mutually exclusive. As is   t h e

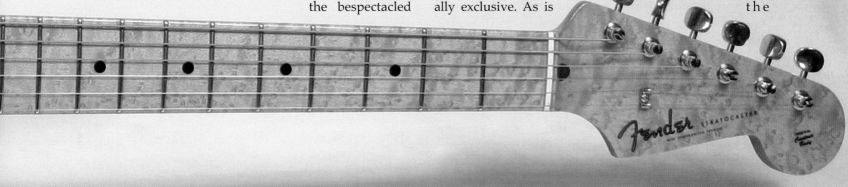

Brit, but this new project was a whole different kettle of fish and chips. Master Builder Greg Fessler hand-built all 54 guitars in the limited run, completing about a half-dozen instruments each month. He reports, "I did a version working with Hank back in the early '90s, but that was a hybrid thing with a few tweaks to suit his personal preferences at the time. This new one was a clone of his factory-stock '59, with several unusual quirks. You have to understand, these guys in the UK are *fanatics* about Hank Marvin [laughs], so the challenge was getting the specs right."

case with other custom colors from the vintage era, Fiesta Red can actually appear in a range of hues. Efficiency trumped consistency at Fender during the 1950s. Guitars were prepped for painting with different undercoats, top coats, and processes, and one stock color was sometimes painted over another stock color before the guitar left the factory, so Fiesta Red guitars from 1959 may have varied a bit to begin with. (Additional discrepancies could arise from the yellowing of top coats, exposure to cigarette smoke or sunlight in a shop window, natural fading, and so on. Sometimes one official Fender color may migrate so drastically over time that it appears to be a different official color.) "I think Hank's Strat was Fiesta Red," says Greg Fessler, "but you have to remember that Fiesta was a little bit all over the place back in the early days, like several other specs. It wasn't dark enough to be Dakota, so I think this particular batch might have simply been slightly different than the other Fiestas we're used to."

Let's remember that regardless of which name Fender might have stuck on this finish, the color itself is the important thing. Howard Gillespie, in *Guitar Buyer*: "I started buying anything that had a flamingo pink color—socks, bric-a-brac, you name it. I'd show the item to Bruce and he'd just say, 'That's not it.' Eventually, Mick Johnson [the luthier who looks after the original 1959 Strat for Bruce Welch] found a color that Bruce was satisfied with. We sprayed it on some wood, and Bruce said, 'That's the most like it I've ever seen.' Bruce phoned Hank in Perth, Australia, and he agreed that a pinkish red was what we were aiming for."

The color of Hank Marvin's flamingo pink/Fiesta red/pinkish red Stratocaster was only one of its distinctive characteristics. Other unique details included a wider nut, a sawed-off trem bar, and a figured bird's-eye neck with rolled edges and asymmetrical contouring—generally a C shape on the treble side, but a D shape on the bass side. Greg Fessler: "Some of the specs were pretty sketchy back in the day. If it looked okay and played okay, then that was fine with them. The nut width is about 1.670", about 20/1000ths over the typical vintage 1.650". The nut and the neck shapes were probably like the color—that's just the way they made it that day. Seeing Hank play, he's holding on to that tremolo bar almost all of the time. That's part of his thing, and that bar is shorter than stock. The three pickups' G-string polepieces are flush, another aberration, but they probably just ran out of the longer ones and borrowed some from the bin. Leo didn't mind that sort of thing all that much, so it might've been, *hey, put whatever we have in there and let's ship some guitars!*"

Regarding the trem, Howard Gillespie explains: "The 'Shadows 50th' became known by Fender as a Dealer Select CRS-59. CRS stood for Custom Red Strat, though many people thought it was code for Cliff Richard Strat. We remembered from the 1992 and 1994 Hank guitars that the bar was very short. This is because Hank or someone else had cut it down (maybe that is why David Gilmour has such a short bar, too), so we asked Fender to replicate it. Greg duplicated that sample. The accessories we put together to go with the CRS had two tremolo bars—the short one Greg did, and a special Easy-Mute, as currently favored by Hank Marvin, made for us by Ian St.John-White at VML [Middlesex, UK], with a uniquely engraved tip pattern. The arm is bent, and positioned parallel to the strings, so palm-muting is much easier. The guitar also had two certificates, one from Fender and one from The Shadows."

The arrival, 1959: "The guitar arrived at a flat shared by Hank, Bruce, and Cliff in Marylebone High Street. When they opened the tweed case, saw the crushed-velvet lining, smelled that smell and saw the pinky-red Strat with bird's-eye maple neck, gold-plated hardware, three pickups and a tremolo arm, no one spoke. No one touched it for a while: They just stared at it. The guitar was the most beautiful thing they'd ever seen. Five years after its creation, this was the first Fender Stratocaster in Britain—an icon."

— from *17 Watts? The Birth of British Rock Guitar*, by Mo Foster

The CRS-59 came with two trem bars. This one is the Easy-Mute, from VML in Middlesex, UK.

Stealthy Hot Rod

The multi-monikered Make'n Music Master Vintage Player Series MVP 1956 Stratocaster Heavy Relic Masterbuilt (whew) was the collaborative brainchild of Master Builder John Cruz and Teddy Gordon, the owner of Chicago-area retailer Make'n Music. It offers a mighty jolt of vintage vibe—nitro-finished ash body with a 2-color sunburst, a quartersawn, V-shaped neck, and a vintage trem. The fingerboard, however, has a 9.5" radius rather than a vintage-era 7.25", the frets are medium jumbos, and the third knob controls tone for both the middle and bridge pickups.

"This is one of those guitars that looks stock but has a bit of hot rodding," John Cruz explains. "I've played a lot of vintage Strats, and I appreciate the history, but let's face it, for me and my style of playing, some of those things like a steeply curved fingerboard and small frets aren't as practical. Teddy wanted things like the [peghead-access]

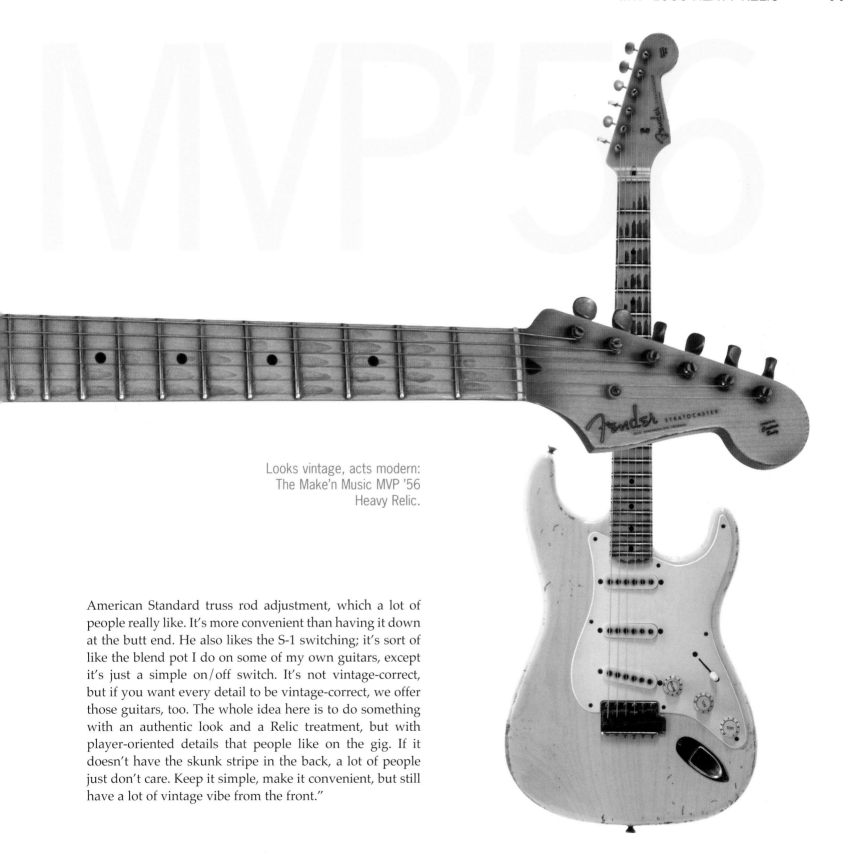

Looks vintage, acts modern:
The Make'n Music MVP '56
Heavy Relic.

American Standard truss rod adjustment, which a lot of people really like. It's more convenient than having it down at the butt end. He also likes the S-1 switching; it's sort of like the blend pot I do on some of my own guitars, except it's just a simple on/off switch. It's not vintage-correct, but if you want every detail to be vintage-correct, we offer those guitars, too. The whole idea here is to do something with an authentic look and a Relic treatment, but with player-oriented details that people like on the gig. If it doesn't have the skunk stripe in the back, a lot of people just don't care. Keep it simple, make it convenient, but still have a lot of vintage vibe from the front."

Custom Shop 1956 Heavy Relic in Desert Sand, a color first used on Fender lap steels and the original pair of student electric Spanish models, the Musicmaster and Duo-Sonic.

Shown here in Sonic Blue, the 2007 LTD 20th Anniversary Master Built Stratocaster celebrated the first two decades of the Custom Shop. Details included a 1966-style headstock, a quartersawn neck, and a Custom Classic trem with a pop-in arm.

One unusual feature was the complement of pickups: a 1969 Custom Shop neck pickup, a 1969 reverse-wound/reverse-polarity middle pickup, and a Texas Special at the bridge.

The first guitar player to go to work for Leo Fender, George Fullerton helped with the design of both the Telecaster and the Stratocaster. He was honored in 2007 with a 150-piece run of the 50th Anniversary George Fullerton 1957 Stratocaster, which was paired with a relic Tweed Pro Junior.

The Master Built Eric Clapton Crossroads Stratocaster was a unique project that raised funds for the Crossroads Centre, the addiction rehab facility founded by Eric Clapton on the Caribbean island of Antigua. It sported a sun-face design based on a drawing by Eric himself and was promptly nicknamed the Sun Strat. The Custom Shop released a limited run of 100 pieces, 50 of them priced at $20,000. The other 50 were paired with a specially badged, sun-faced Crossroads '57 Twin Amp and sold for $30,000. All proceeds went to the Crossroads Centre.

Yngwie

If you're going to belt out slash-and-pillage lyrics like "I'm a Viking, by my sword you will die," you can't just play any old guitar. At age 15, future Swedish metal overlord Yngwie Malmsteen selected a 1971 Olympic White Stratocaster. He "scalloped" the fingerboard, gouging out the wood between the frets in such a way that the strings, when depressed, would touch the frets but not the board underneath. He inflicted additional modifications, stuck a "Play Loud" sticker on it, thrashed it, and played it hard on many gigs and recordings before retiring it in 1992. The Fender served him well, as he proved that he was no ordinary headbanger but was instead a gifted virtuoso capable not only of preternatural fingerboard flash but also, when he feels like it, exquisite flights of melody.

The Custom Shop released several scallop-board Malmsteen models. By the mid-2000s, the shop's tooling, techniques, and finesse had evolved to a point where a Tribute clone seemed challenging, to be sure, but feasible. After John Cruz and Mike Eldred visited the flamboyant metal virtuoso at his home in Miami to spec out his disfigured guitar, the Master Builders got to work. Jason Smith described

Yngwie's Strat as "one of the most beat-to-crap guitars I've ever seen in my life. That thing had seen a lot of abuse."

Released in November 2008, the "Play Loud" Yngwie Malmsteen Tribute Stratocaster was a meticulous recreation of Yngwie's original '71. Among its many quirks, the Tribute's tone controls are disconnected, so that the signal runs directly from the pickups to the jack (as on Neil Young's "Old Black" Les Paul). John Cruz: "The Oly White finish had yellowed over the years. The biggest challenge was getting the finish to look right, with the color match, the cracks, and all the detailed dings, bite marks, even burns."

Cruz described the scalloping on Yngwie's personal guitar as "crude, not too pretty." Regarding the fingerboard on the Tribute's prototype, he explained: "I copied the exact depth of the original, including all the file marks and scattered sanding that came from Yngwie's own hand." Jason Smith: "If there are places on that fingerboard where it's uneven and worn, we duplicated it on the Tributes. We are not trying to make this a perfectly symmetrical fingerboard. That's not what this Tribute is about. It's about duplicating for you, the customer, Yngwie Malmsteen's personal guitar."

Left:
Eric Clapton was Fender's first signature artist. His endorsement was key to the company's success in the post-CBS era, and he remains its most prominent endorser ever. In 2004, the Custom Shop unveiled its own version of the Clapton Strat, shown here with a Daphne Blue finish, Vintage Noiseless pickups, and various refinements.

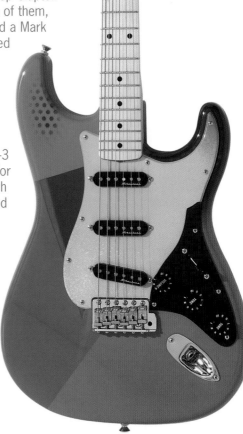

Right:
Graffiti/street art pioneer John "Crash" Matos painted a number of Strat bodies for Eric Clapton. Most of Eric's "Crashocasters" were basically Custom Shop Clapton models, but one of them, Crash-3, featured a Mark Kendrick-designed control plate in black anodized metal, a detail borrowed from George Fullerton's personal '54 Strat; Crash-3 sold at auction for $321,000. Crash then hand-painted 50 bodies for a limited run of Custom Shop Strats built by Master Builder Todd Krause, all of them featuring the Kendrick/Fullerton top plate.

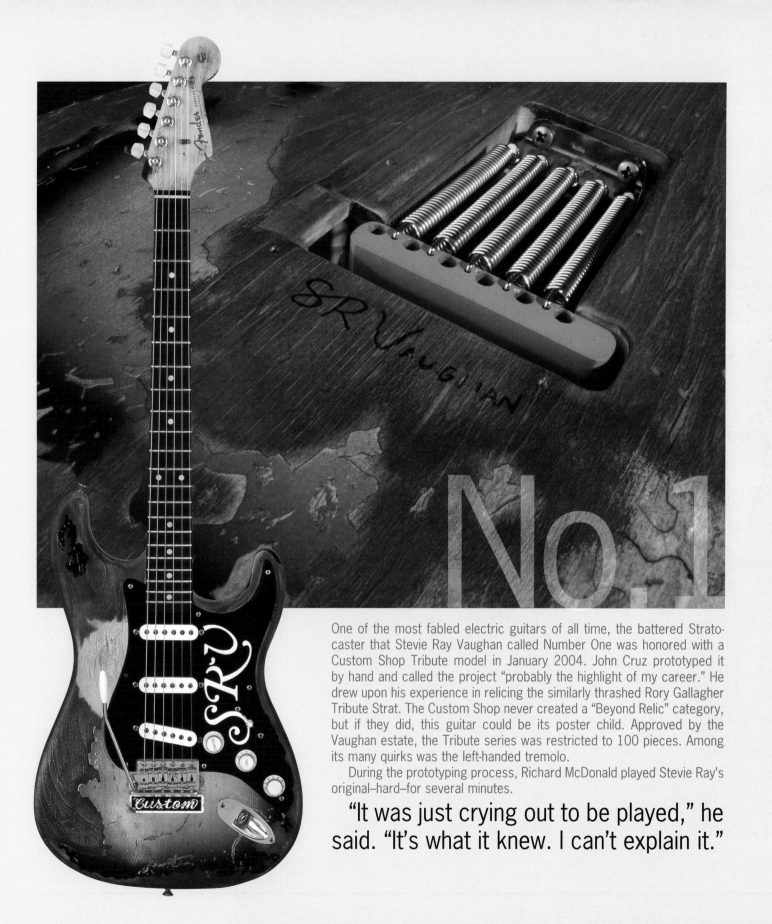

One of the most fabled electric guitars of all time, the battered Stratocaster that Stevie Ray Vaughan called Number One was honored with a Custom Shop Tribute model in January 2004. John Cruz prototyped it by hand and called the project "probably the highlight of my career." He drew upon his experience in relicing the similarly thrashed Rory Gallagher Tribute Strat. The Custom Shop never created a "Beyond Relic" category, but if they did, this guitar could be its poster child. Approved by the Vaughan estate, the Tribute series was restricted to 100 pieces. Among its many quirks was the left-handed tremolo.

During the prototyping process, Richard McDonald played Stevie Ray's original—hard—for several minutes.

"It was just crying out to be played," he said. "It's what it knew. I can't explain it."

The Rory Gallagher Tribute Stratocaster of 2004 re-created a guitar that rivaled Stevie Ray Vaughan's Number One and Yngwie Malmsteen's "Play Loud" Strat in terms of wear and wounding inflicted by hard rockin' road warriors. It spent some time in the Custom Shop, where it acquired virtual holy relic status. Mike Eldred: "It was a big honor just to hold something that such a great artist had played so much blazing music on." John Cruz: "One night after everybody went home I plugged it in and really cranked it. What a great experience to play that guitar. It's really rewarding to know that all of our hard work pays off, and people will be able to share a bit of that legacy. It was a tough project, but I think we nailed it pretty damn close. All the templates made up for it are still in use today. We still get orders for it." Cruz hand-built 40 Tribute Stratocasters for the European market, precisely duplicating the original's accumulated scarring and somehow conjuring its decades-long journey of performance intensity.

Lenny

SRV's Other 6-String Treasure

The Custom Shop's Lenny guitar was named after
Stevie Ray Vaughan's wife Lenora and the beautiful
song he composed for her late one night. The young,
broke Stephen Ray Vaughan had discovered a 1965
Strat in an Austin pawnshop and fell in love with it
but couldn't afford its $350 price. Lenora recruited
seven friends who believed in Stevie's talents and
donated $50 each. They purchased the guitar and
presented it to a delighted Stevie on his 26th birthday, October 3, 1980.

The guitar had originally been finished with a
3-color sunburst but was later covered rather ama-
teurishly with a dark natural stain. Stevie replaced
its rosewood-board neck with a Charvel maple neck
that was given to him by Billy Gibbons. The trem
was modified so that Stevie could pull up as well as
push down on the bar, facilitating the rollercoaster
whammy swoops often heard at the close of the guitar's namesake song. The back of the guitar was auto-
graphed by Mickey Mantle at the Astrodome in
April 1985, after Stevie had performed "The
Star Spangled Banner" on it (he'd learned
the anthem on the car ride to the stadium).

In 2004, Guitar Center acquired the
guitar for $623,500 and commissioned
Fender to reproduce a limited run of Lenny
Tributes. The $17,000 Tribute was unveiled
on December 12, 2007, meticulously recreating the original's many quirks. No Team
Built versions were offered; all were crafted
by Master Builders with the assistance of
apprentices. Each guitar was personally
overseen by Master Builder Jason Smith,
who spearheaded the project. One it's-a-
small-world connection: The original's
replacement neck was not a Fender, but
it had been built and signed years before
by the Custom Shop's Mike Eldred when
he worked at Charvel.

Jeff Beck Signature Guitar

In January 2004 the Custom Shop premiered its own take on the Jeff Beck Signature Stratocaster. Details included a contoured heel, Noiseless pickups, an LSR roller nut, and a bit of rewiring (the knobs are Volume, Tone for the front pickup, and Tone for the middle and bridge pickups—a sensible increase in practicality for any 3-knob Strat).

Robin Trower

Todd Krause worked with Robin Trower in 2004 to craft two versions of Team Built, Trower-approved Stratocasters. The Team Built Custom Tribute was modeled after a stock '73/'74 Strat like the one Trower had played on *Bridge Of Sighs*, while the Team Built Signature had a 4-bolt/ bullet-rod neck, Sperzel keys, and abalone inlays. The Tribute's "Custom" designation reflected the builders' deeper level of personal attention.

Mark Kendrick's Bound-Board Master Design

The Master Design concept was a way to open up Custom Shop territory between the relatively affordable Team Built guitars and the exclusive top-of-the-line models. Each Master Builder was given the go-ahead to build his own dream guitar. He would personally craft a handful of Master Built examples—as few as 10—and then the shop would create several dozen additional versions at a somewhat reduced price. In 2004, Mark Kendrick responded with enthusiasm, recreating a 1965 Stratocaster whose bound fingerboard made it one of the rarest of all cataloged Fenders from the vintage era. Finished in Lake Placid Blue over Olympic White, it offered Closet Classic aging, an L serial number, a special case, and a trove of case-candy extras.

Mark explains that on a vintage Fender, having one color sprayed over another is "a pretty good indication that the body was reworked in the factory. In other words, the Oly White didn't make it through the first time. By the time it went through for a second pass, production requirements had changed. In my observation, this practice was more prevalent during the CBS [1965-1985] era but did happen through the FEI [the earlier Fender Electric Instruments] era as well. Also, all alder bodies were prepared for sunburst, as it was the most popular color at the time. Consequently, under the Oly White, the original 1965 Strat I modeled the guitar after was prepped accordingly. [Painting the Lake Placid Blue over white] makes no difference in the final result. It was strictly for authenticity."

The Custom Shop's '66 Strat NOS (New Old Stock) was added to the Time Machine line in 2004. Although the original was a CBS Fender guitar, the acknowledged decline in Fender products took a while to kick in. Several guitars and amps from the early CBS era are highly regarded. The guitar shown here is finished in a beautiful Teal Green.

Evoking mid-'50s Fender literature and a Route 66 time-warp road trip, the Memorabilia Set paired a 1956 Relic Strat crafted by Master Builder Chris Fleming with a Pro Junior amplifier. Also called the Art Deco set, the $15,999 duo was conceived and adorned by Arizona-based artist Dave Newman.

Gold on Blonde

The Mary Kaye

In one of the most famous of the mid-'50s promo photos, Mary Kaye, the queen of the Las Vegas lounge scene, was pictured with a 1956 Stratocaster, serial number 09391. It was not her main guitar. In fact, she did not own the instrument at all. An accomplished jazz guitarist, she played and treasured an archtop that John D'Angelico had personally built for her. But she did like the Twin amplifier that also appeared in the photo, and she agreed to Don Randall's request to hold the newfangled solidbody when she posed for the now-iconic image.

The Mary Kaye Stratocaster was added to the Custom Shop Tribute series in January 2005. All 60 pieces of the original run were personally built over a one-year period by Greg Fessler, recreating what might be called Fender's first and only unofficial "artist" guitar. The model was suggested by this author. I pointed out that Fender's most famous pickup winder, the legendary Abigail Ybarra, joined the Fender team in 1956, the same year the Mary Kaye Trio photo was first published. Women are all too rare in the lore of American vintage guitars, and I thought it might be appropriate to honor Mary Kaye with a guitar whose pickups would be specially wound by Abigail. Looking back in 2014, Greg Fessler commented: "That was another one of those really successful guitars. I probably could have made a lot more of them, but we wanted to keep everything limited."

Each Tribute featured a straight-grain maple neck with a period-correct 7.25" radius, vintage-style frets, Ybarra-wound pickups, and the defining characteristics of gold hardware and a semi-transparent White Blonde nitrocellulose finish over a straight-grain ash body. While other Tributes were either entirely new models or clones of an iconic artist's highly personalized guitar, the Mary Kaye was unique in that it replicated a stock, cataloged item from the vintage era. It was unique in another way as well. Fender has had a slew of artist Strats—Claptons, SRVs, Eric Johnsons—but "Mary Kaye" was a common nickname for white/gold Strats for decades before the Custom Shop made it official. Ms. Kaye told this author that for many years she was unaware of her fame in vintage circles until she walked into a music store one day and was told, "You are in all the guitar books."

Freak Flag High

The Reverse Hendrix Proto Strat

The original Top Scoop Strat of 1979-1980, also called the "Hendrix Reverse Proto" guitar, was somewhat legendary—but not for the usual reasons. With its reverse headstock, it was one of several Fenders intended to evoke the ephemeral magic of Jimi Hendrix. If you didn't look too closely, it did bear a passing resemblance to Jimi's upside-down, right-handed '68, but truth be told, the original "Hendrix prototype" had no significant connection to Jimi Hendrix, and it wasn't much of a prototype, either. Despite its "Prototype" stamp, it did not predate a production guitar that Fender ever built, or even intended to build. It was a vanity project dreamed up by a sales guy and dumped on Custom Shop co-founder John Page seven or eight years before the shop was established; Page was working in R&D at the time.

This rare bird/odd duck reversed the locations of the tummy tuck (now on the front, hence the Top Scoop nickname) and the armrest (now, inexplicably, on the back). Neither served any function except to make the guitar unique. Informed speculation varies as to how many were built. Early estimates of 25 were likely a bit inflated; the number was probably about 15. Despite features that might charitably be described as "eccentric," the model was still an ultra-rare, stock Stratocaster, which made rumors and speculation all but inevitable. A photo of Stevie Ray Vaughan playing one as well as reports that John Mayer was trying to acquire all of the originals pumped enough mystique into the atmosphere to justify reanimating the creature in the Custom Shop.

Dennis Galuszka took on the project in 2005 and built 100 replicas over a two-year period. All were finished in Closet Classic Vintage White. As if it weren't off-kilter enough, the guitar had an additional quirk: right-side-up decals on the upside-down headstock.

Maligned for its impractical contouring yet held in affection for its forehead-slapper idiosyncrasies, the guitar may have had an overlooked benefit, at least in the minds of a few discriminating players and builders. Dennis Galuszka believes that the increased tension of its longer-length bass strings gave it more of a robust, piano-like bottom end, while the shorter treble strings were easier to bend.

With its body covered in white gold leaf, the Master Salute Stratocaster of 2005 was one of the most challenging projects ever undertaken by the Custom Shop. John Cruz built the prototype and reported: "We applied the gold leaf with a varnish. The leaves were housed in a little square box with tissue paper in between each leaf. They were smaller than cocktail napkins and very thin. The whole process was *very* exacting and time-consuming." The builders used special tools to apply the leaves because touching them with their hands could leave ruinous finger-oil deposits. With a soft-sheen metallic finish that was actually closer to silver in color, the Master Salute Stratocasters retailed for $8,226.

The Carved Phoenix Stratocaster of 2005 offered tour-de-force woodcarving on an ultra-deluxe Stratocaster. Appointments included ingot-like gold pickup covers, gold hardware, and a fingerboard inlaid with mother of pearl and silver wire. Yuriy Shishkov built it. He reports: "I was limited to building a great instrument, making sure the playability and all functional details were correct. I had some input on the pickguard, inlay, and overall artistic quality, but it's George Amicay who gets the credit for the amazing figured-maple woodcarving."

The Strat Pro descended from the price-sheet instruments of the early 1990s in that it combined "the most requested modifications that the Custom Shop has offered over the last 20 years." While individual details had appeared on other guitars, the new combination was unique and eminently practical. Features included Samarium Cobalt Noiseless pickups, an LSR roller nut, American Standard frets, a bend-friendly 12" radius, a contoured neck heel for upper-register comfort, a 2-point trem, and staggered, locking tuners. Later versions, like this one, replaced the LSR with a conventional nut. This author wrote in 2011: "It is simply one of the great workhorse guitars of all time."

Yet another category in the Custom Shop's mid-2000s catalog was the Builder Select designation, which gave each Master Builder the freedom to do pretty much whatever he wanted. In late 2005, John Cruz built 100 1962-style Stratocasters in Sonic Blue with a Heavy Relic treatment. Features included a 9.5" fingerboard radius, mint-green pickguard, S-1 switching, and an American Vintage trem. It was a classic example of a common approach: vintage vibe meets versatile wiring and a bend-friendly fingerboard.

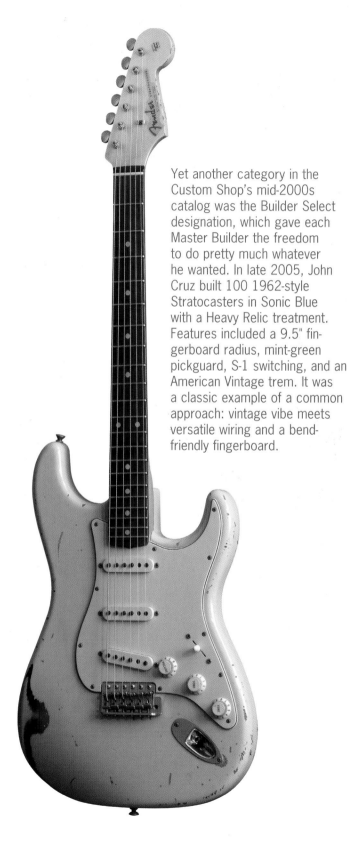

The second Master Design Stratocaster was John English's '59 Strat Relic in Sonic Blue, introduced in 2005.

It seems almost every Strat player has at one time or another fantasized about a perfect combo of features. The Master Builders certainly have. While most mix-and-match Strats recombine existing bits from other guitars, John Cruz' Builder Select '61 Stratocaster Relic was more of a departure. He reported: "The whole idea was, this is my take on doing a hot Strat with a wider nut, which a lot of people were requesting from me anyway on my one-offs. I did a 1.75" nut, really wide, and not traditional for a Strat." Other details included a DiMarzio Tone Zone humbucker and a pair of single-coils that John co-designed with Abigail Ybarra. The wiring was unconventional as well: The S-1 switch now coil-tapped the humbucker, and John replaced the third knob with a fader that blended the bridge and neck pickups.

The La Florita set of 2005 combined a hardtail Strat built by Chris Fleming with a Blues Junior amp. The Mexican blanket motif of the amp is a lovely complement to the South Of The Border iconography of the guitar. Both pieces of the $14,999 set were painted by guitarist Kid Ramos.

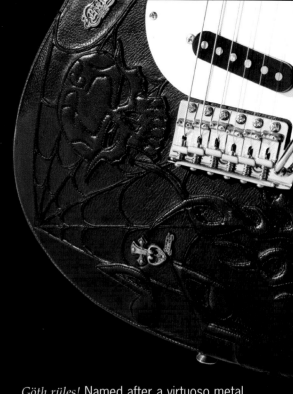

Göth rüles! Named after a virtuoso metal guitarist from Japan, the Michiya Haruhata BWL Stratocaster of 2005 was offered in two versions, both adorned by master silversmith and leather artist Bill Wall of Bill Wall Leather, or BWL, in Malibu. John English hand-crafted a dozen Master Built guitars wrapped with heavily tooled black leather; their skull and spiderweb motifs were tempered with rather cheery musical notes. The 60 Team Built versions featured a massive locking trem and hand-engraved metal knobs, pickguards, and jack plates, plus a weighty Iron Cross for an extra Teutonic/occult vibe.

Recreating An Icon

The Blackie Project

In the introduction to this book's original edition, Eric Clapton recalled acquiring several '50s Stratocasters in a Nashville shop. "They were so out of fashion you could pick up a perfectly genuine Strat for 200 dollars or 300 dollars–even less!" He gave one to Steve Winwood, one to George Harrison, and one to Pete Townshend. He took apart the guitars he kept for himself and assembled his favorite bits. The result was a black-bodied parts guitar. He called it "Blackie … a hybrid, a mongrel." It would become his primary studio and stage instrument for 15 years or more, achieving iconic status as one of the most famous electric guitars of all time.

Clapton put Blackie up for sale to raise money for the Crossroads Centre, the nonprofit addiction treatment facility he founded in 1998. It was offered at Christie's New York auction house on June 24, 2004. As deep-pocket collectors phoned in from around the world, the wildfire bidding escalated from $100,000 to $800,000 in less than 30 seconds, accompanied by what one auction-house spokesman described as "outbursts of devotional excitement." When the smoke cleared, Blackie had been acquired by Guitar Center for $959,500.

By 2006, the Custom Shop was nearing the end of its second decade, now with a long track record of producing to-die-for instruments. When word hit the street that the shop would recreate a limited run of the Blackie Strat, an urgent buzz coursed through vintage circles and retail chains. The new model would be the Custom Shop's most anticipated guitar.

Blackie arrived in Corona on October 24, 2005. Todd Krause was the logical choice to spearhead the project, having already built several guitars for Eric Clapton. When asked what it was like holding a million-dollar guitar, he replied, "It didn't feel like a million-dollar guitar. It was just *the* guitar. The dollar value was not what I felt in it. What I saw and felt was the history, and the kind of personality you get in a guitar when the same person plays it for so long." Once Eric and his guitar tech, Lee Dickson, signed off on Todd's prototype, the Master Builders set to work, crafting 275 Tribute Series Blackie Stratocasters over a period of several months. They duplicated the original's multiple scratches, dings, and cigarette burns, even the

worn areas that came from Clapton's own hand after many years of rigorous playing on stage and in the studio. (The only details not duplicated were areas that were so worn they diminished the guitar's playability.)

Because Blackie had been put together from different instruments in the first place, and was then disassembled, resanded, refinished, repaired, and reassembled with parts from different guitars, the builders faced a host of technical challenges. Nevertheless, the Tribute was a stunning success. Despite the suggested retail price of an eye-poppin' $24,000, the 106-piece run sold out in the first two minutes of "Black Friday," November 24, 2006.

Blackie

Greg Fessler built this guitar for a 2006 NAMM show. It re-creates the Stratoburst finish, which fades from silver into sapphire blue. The unusual color was complemented with satin nickel hardware and pickups of Fessler's own design. "I have a picture of that guitar on my wall," he says. "It's one of my favorites. I thought that was something that people would really dig, but I never got many orders for them. The silver and blue one turned up in Japan. There were other original 'Stratoburst' color combinations in the early '80s, like red and gold or bronze, so I may try another one."

The fourth member of the Master Design program was Greg Fessler's gold sparkle Stratocaster of 2006, an $8,000 guitar. He hand-built 100 examples, and then oversaw another 100 Team Built versions that retailed for $5,000. His goal was a traditional Fender "with a bit more flash." Greg Fessler: "Those things got a lot of attention and were so popular. I backed off from making them because we wanted to keep it exclusive, but I really think that if I had made 500, Fender could have sold them all."

Premium Vintage

A bright finish with a soupçon of twang . . .

One trend in recent years has been Fender's partnering with other companies, several of them luxury brands. When asked if there is such a thing as a Fender life-style, then-CEO Larry Thomas responded in 2012: "Sure. Harley-Davidson—it's not about the motorcycles. It's about freedom; it's about the open air, the adventure of the open road, all those things in life. The motorcycle is just a vehicle to get you there. Fender, it's not about the guitar. It's about the music. It's about people who want to be part of the scene, who want to create, who want to rock and roll. It's about the emotional connection. We're not just about building great tools for musicians. I'm about a global lifestyle brand. We can license people who make apparel, and then you can see our brand on premium audio systems in cars, maybe headphones, lots of things."

The Custom Shop had already moved in this direction, associating Fender's 60th anniversary with a premium winemaker, the Hill Family Estate of California's Napa Valley. After several tastings, a Fender-approved Presidential Blend of cabernet and merlot was crafted and bottled six to a case. The cases were made of figured tone woods and decorated like fancy guitars, with inlays and trim of abalone, rosewood, maple, and ebony. In 2006, Fender commissioned the Custom Shop to build 100 special Stratocasters as part of the package. Each one featured gold hardware, knock-out woods, mother-of-pearl dots, and a pearl-inlaid 60th Anniversary logo on the fingerboard. Each AAA flame-maple top was hand-stained with grape must from the winery; the color was dubbed Hill Harvest Red.

One of the Custom Shop's most beautiful Stratocasters, the 2010 Q1 (1st Quarter) Limited 1958 Stratocaster Relic achieved its distinctive look with a Candy Apple Red paint and a nitro lacquer finish over a gold undercoat. A gold anodized pickguard, tinted-lacquer neck, black dots, and the relic treatment complete the look. The neck contour is a big ol' 10/56 V, and the fingerboard is a 9.5". Pickups hand-wound by Abigail Ybarra.

Leo Fender surely would have scratched his head in wonderment to learn that one day his name-sake company would sell a dozen officially sanctioned Strato-casters adorned with fascist poster graphics that hinted of Orwellian overlord paranoia. With more than a whiff of wink-wink hipster irony and stencil/street-art chic, the guitars were built by Todd Krause and painted and signed by Shepard Fairey, arguably the most famous graphic artist ever to be associated with the Custom Shop.

The VG Stratocaster integrated Roland's COSM (Composite Object Sound Modeling) technology into a modified American Standard Strat. Fender offered it from 2007 to 2009, and Roland reintroduced it in 2013. While limited compared to today's guitar/software applications, the VG, or G-5A in Roland parlance, was nevertheless a practical leap forward in versatility. Aside from Fender's standard Strat sounds and pickup combinations, the VG/G-5A electronics offered a variety of gig-worthy, virtual alternatives—Telecaster, 12-string, baritone, humbucking sounds, five acoustic guitars, and several alternate tunings.

Justin Norvell: "A primary concept was to offer 'Fender elegant simplicity' in a versatile instrument. Where most tech products come full of features and potential, they also come with a massive manual that could require an engineering degree. We wanted to 'un-daunt' the process, so it was just two extra knobs that opened up a whole world of options—super simple, and usable. We didn't just put Roland's tech into our guitar. We put our teams together and spent days tweaking and sculpting the tones to be 'Fender Approved.'"